IN HIS TIME

Written at God's prompting:
Memories and lessons in coming to be saved and
learning to trust in and walk daily with the Lord

Mary Ann Zadra

In His Time by Mary Ann Zadra

Copyright 2013, Mary Ann Zadra

ISBN 978-1-300-51554-8

First Edition printed December 2012 via Lulu.com
Second Edition printed July 2013 via Lulu.com
by Zadra Concern, West Saint Paul Minnesota, a division of
Zadco Incorporated Worldwide

*Presented with love and delight by Tony and Cree Zadra of
the Zadra Concern to our favorite Mary Ann!*

Once upon a time...

When I was a child I would become excited when I would pick up a book and read the beginning words, "Once upon a time..." because I knew that a wonderful story was about to begin. We all reflect on our lives and recall moments that have occurred "once upon a time." I have done it myself hundreds of times as I have brought up stories of past experiences to share with family and friends.

"Once upon a time" I felt led by the Lord to write down things that happened to me since I invited Christ into my life to be my Lord and Savior. I was obedient and I did just that—a little book of sorts—with lessons learned, family events, God's words to me. Then it was finished. "Once upon a time" I took the finished writing and put it in a drawer—and forgot about it for years.

Today, while rummaging through a drawer, there with an accumulation of many things, I found it. It has been so long since I looked at it—was it even worth keeping? What in the world did I even write? I sat down at two o'clock this afternoon and opened up to page one...

...It is now six o'clock and I have finished. It has been a walk down memory lane for me and a time to reflect, smile, and even shed tears as I read over so many things that happened in my life "once upon a time."

It seems odd to me to share the things I wrote all these years later. Yet, I feel compelled to do just that—my feeble attempt to give you an insight into some of the things that I experienced walking with the Lord who does everything just right, and brings all things to pass "in His time."

"From this day I will bless you"
Haggai 2:18-19

July 24, 1976—My eleventh wedding anniversary. I quickly got out of bed and put on my robe. I could hear Chet and the boys busily messing up the kitchen as they invented whatever for breakfast. *Thank You, Jesus, for Chet. Thank You for the way he cares for me. Thank You for the long sleep I was able to get because he got up with the boys. Thank You, Lord, for these wonderful eleven years.*

I quietly tiptoed up the steps. *Oh, please, Lord, don't let them know I'm up yet. I want one minute with You before this day gets underway, just one quick peek in the Bible, Lord, a little food for thought to carry me through the day.* I reached for my Living Bible and opened it. I put my finger down and looked—there, right at the tip of my finger, in II Kings 25:3, right on page 333, there it was: July 24. I had never seen a date in the Bible before, yet, here was today's date at my fingertip in God's own Word. I moved my finger up and it fell on the words, "eleventh year." Today was my eleventh wedding anniversary! I read the whole paragraph, II Kings 25:1-3, but it made no sense. It seemed that God was concerned with showing me only the dates and numbers in this passage. There was one more date: March 25 of the ninth year. *Where was I then, Lord, in the 9th year of my marriage?* I felt impressed to look in the front of the Bible. There I recorded on March 25, 1974, the day I began my walk with the Lord. I was so excited by this time—I whispered, "Lord, what does this all mean? Are You simply acknowledging my wedding anniversary, or are You trying to tell me something?" I grabbed a bunch of pages and turned them over finding myself in Haggai 2. I began to read,

> "But now note this: From today, this 24th day of the month, as the foundation of the Lord's temple is finished and from this day onward, I will bless you. Notice, I am giving you this promise now before you have even begun to build the Temple Structure, and before you have harvested your grain, and before the grapes and figs and pomegranates and olives have produced their next crops. From this day I will bless you." Haggai 2:18-19

I read the Scripture over and over again. I was overwhelmed at the dates I read and the message of blessing. I felt that the Lord was speaking directly to me. I had come seeking a word to begin my day and I read a promise of blessing beginning on this day and lasting forever—a promise that I felt was just for me—me—who only two and a half years ago did not even know the Lord personally, or even believed deeply and sincerely that He absolutely without a doubt existed—me—who for some 30 plus years thought that there was a God but He was to be saved for eternity or called upon in case of extreme emergency—me—who said "I believe" but it was head knowledge—and deep down I felt that I was in control of all of the circumstances of my life—me—the sinner—that me!

No, Lord, not that me—not for the last two and a half years, for I have not been the same, but the person I have become because of you.

Thank You, Jesus, for Your blessing, for Your promise, for Your presence, for Your kindness and compassion, for the deep peace and joy that comes only from You. Thank You, Jesus, for Your precious blood. Thank You that You were my substitute on Calvary's cross. Thank You that You paid the debt of my sin. Thank You for forgiving me and helping me through the changes in my life.

"For all have sinned and fall short of the glory of God."
Romans 3:23

Only, I never knew that. Since I was a little girl, I had been taught by loving parents and friends how to behave, act, and treat others. I had been instructed in what was right and what was wrong. It was right to go to church. It was right to be kind and helpful and responsible. I had a proper religious training, and I learned a wealth of facts about God. God made us, God is good, God is all-loving and all-knowing, God is three persons in one. I even recall talking to God as I skipped home from school.

But, at the same time I was learning about God, I was learning everything else which was certainly more exciting and interesting to me. Someday, I would take time to learn more about God, about the church I attended, the religion I was part of, but not now when there were so many other things I had to do. Periodically, I would feel a deep sense that God was important and I would feel drawn to church. For a time in high school, I would run into the church across the street from the school just to talk to God; but by the time I went to college, I attended church services only because I felt that I had to. I knew it would disappoint my parents if I didn't go, and frankly, I was afraid not to because I might be doing something wrong.

After I was married, I went to church every Sunday. Chet came with me at first, but then he stopped. I remember going alone and crying in church. I was more concerned that Chet didn't want to come with me than I was about the reason I should have been there. I went out of stubbornness. I wanted Chet to feel neglected when I trotted off alone, but he never seemed the least bit affected. Chet was raised by a Catholic father and a Methodist mother—he was taken to both churches and even attended occasional services at The Salvation Army. I know that he carried a Bible when he went into the service, but I doubt if he ever opened it. Before we were married he took instructions and became a Catholic. He was baptized and made his first communion. I think we both knew it was just a procedure that he went through to please me, who wanted to please my parents. Mission accomplished—they were truly pleased. We were no closer to God because of it, and before long,

Chet became bored with church and stopped going altogether. I kept going, but it was a chore. I couldn't pray; the hour seemed like five; and I daydreamed my way through the service.

I welcomed my first pregnancy. It brought with it my first acceptable excuse for not attending church. I would feel giddy and my stomach would turn when I sat in a room so full of people. I had myself believing that I would go back as soon as the baby came. In the meantime, I would sit at home and pray the rosary. After Tony was born in 1969 I had a new excuse—I was too busy with a new baby. That was in September. By November, my excuse had changed to icy roads and driving too far to town. Just when I was running out of excuses, I became ill and the doctor told me that I had all the symptoms of rheumatoid arthritis. A trip to Mayo Clinic confirmed that I did indeed have arthritis, however, not rheumatoid. They started me on a program of rest and taking aspirins. At the time I was really miserable, but looking back, I realize that I got all the mileage out of my condition that I could. Everyone waited on me hand and foot, and I loved it. Whenever I needed a little attention, I could rely on my aches and pains to get it. I showed no mercy to anyone around, especially Chet.

In 1972 I was pregnant again—another boy, David. I had felt pretty good during my pregnancy but was extremely tired. After Dave was born, I went back to my aspirins and never passed up an opportunity to tell everyone about my arthritis.

"Behold, I stand at the door and knock..."
Revelation 3:20

David was born a week before Christmas. I remember that Christmas because it was wonderful. I had just gotten home from the hospital and it was our first Christmas alone without a lot of running, relatives, and confusion. It was special because it was the family Christmas that I wanted. Chet gave me a huge Bible. I had asked for one for a year, thinking that every home should have one. I tried several times to get into the habit of reading it, but none of it really seemed to appeal to me beyond the Christmas story and Noah's ark. Oh, well, I thought, I'd keep a good record in the front and pass it on to my grandchildren when I was old. All during this period, I prayed the rosary, 15 minutes a day for 54 days, then I'd stop for a few weeks and start another 54 day Novena (27 days in petition, 27 days in Thanksgiving). My mother had always prayed the rosary, and I thought that if I did that daily, counted in the two or three special holidays I attended mass, I would be doing pretty good. My devotion was centered on Mary, and although I read passages of our Lord's life in a booklet I had, my thoughts were centered on Mary.

During this period, we built a new home, and in 1973 we moved in. The house was my dream house—huge, every room oversized and equipped with everything including central vacuuming, a garbage compactor, and a Strauss Crystal chandelier in the master bedroom. We knew that the house was far from what we wanted it to be—no carpets, curtains, and an unfinished basement—but our plan was that we would live in it until we retired, so we had ample time to make it the palace I envisioned. I wanted to have expensive furniture, fancy decorations, a great car parked outside, and a wardrobe to match. I was anxious to have everything done immediately, but we had extended ourselves already and I had to grit my teeth and admit that we would have to put off buying furniture and draperies for a while.

I often wonder how things would have turned out in my life if I did not answer the door... "Behold, I stand at the door and knock. If any man hear my voice and open the door, I will come in and sup with him and he with me." (Revelation 3:20)

We were pretty settled in the new house, though there were a million things to do. The kids loved it! David was playpen-sized, but Tony had what seemed like acres to play. Although most of my day was busy, I found that every afternoon when the boys napped, I had some free time. I was so addicted to soap operas that I would watch several hours of uninterrupted television. I would tell everyone that I ironed or folded clothes or did some serious cleaning while I watched, but truthfully, I sat on the couch absorbed by the shows. I decided that if I had a hobby I could work at while I watched the soaps, I'd have that as an excuse.

Just exactly at that time, I received a catalogue in the mail from a library in a nearby city. They were beginning a mail-a-book program for country residents who were unable to use the library facilities. I decided that reading was the perfect hobby and looked over the list of available books. I wanted love stories, or mysteries, or even science fiction, but there wasn't a single title that appealed to me. Then I looked in the religious section and saw a book by Pat Boone called "A New Song." I was curious about an entertainer writing a book, so I selected that one.

I don't recall the other books I selected, but in the months to come, I read just about every book I could get my hands on from the religious section. I couldn't stop myself—I got so absorbed in my new hobby, I forgot all about television, and weeks began to go by without turning the TV on. When I read all of the books that the mail library had, the librarian sent me a note indicating that she had books in her personal library that I could read and she would inquire if libraries in other places were willing to send books. One week I got 23 books, and eight another week. Manila padded envelopes piled up all around the house from many libraries—some as far as 200 miles away. I confess that I never read all of those books, but I read enough to see that these people had experiences that were out of the ordinary. They had a real joy for life, and living was a miracle. It all centered around the person of Jesus Christ and I wanted what they had. All of a sudden, I had an overwhelming desire to know this Jesus personally, as a friend, the way all of these people did. I had no idea that I was about to answer that knocking at my door.

Born Again

One day when I was reading a book by Billy Graham I came to a section that contained a prayer of commitment. I knelt down on my uncarpeted floor in my unpainted bedroom, leaning on the old bedspread I longed to replace and prayed that prayer. I prayed something like this: "Lord, Jesus, I need You. I receive You as my Savior and Lord. I open up the door of my life to You, Jesus, and invite You to take control of the throne of my life. Make me the kind of person You want me to be. I know that I am a sinner, Lord, and I need Your forgiveness. I turn from my sins. I want to trust You as Savior and follow You as Lord."

All of a sudden, tears were streaming down my face and I felt so wonderful. I felt so clean, so at peace, and I knew, I *knew* that Jesus was real. He was alive and He was now living in me. I knew that I had been touched by the living God and the room was suddenly the most beautiful place I'd ever been. It was several days before it dawned on me that I was a new person.

"But to all who receive Him, He gave the right to become children of God. All they needed to do was trust Him to save them. All those who believe this are reborn." (John 1:12-13)

The next day, I re-prayed the prayer, and the next, and the next. I had obtained a Bible that had a message in it from Bill Bright. He explained that once Jesus is in our lives, *He Is In!* We aren't to depend on feelings, but on faith and fact. I realized that I was depending on my feelings, and when my "high" feeling didn't last, I thought that Jesus was no longer there. I am so grateful to the Lord for being so patient and gentle with me and for leading me into the truth and the blessed assurance that He will never leave me or forsake me. (Hebrews 13:5)

Slowly, as the days went by, I began to notice changes in myself. Not big dramatic events, but definite changes. One day I suddenly realized that I no longer swore. I was really terrible, giving no thought to the language I used or how unbecoming it was. I never prayed about it, it just left me. I saw that God was beginning to "clean house". He was sweeping out the dust and dirt—letting out the old musty smell, and letting the "Son" shine in.

I knew that I was saved, born again. I also knew that I had done nothing to earn this gift, it was given to me by a loving and wonderful Father. "For by the grace are you saved through faith; and that not of yourselves; it is a gift of God, not of works, lest any man should boast." (Ephesians 2:8-9) I was part of God's family, and He confirmed it to me in a wonderful way.

On Easter Sunday, 1974, I attended church. It was the custom to bring a basket of food to be blessed so it could be shared by the family on Easter Sunday after mass. It had been a long time since I had come to church and the first time since I had invited Christ into my heart. I couldn't get over all of the noise I heard as I entered the doors. I could hear laughter and voices—it sounded like a big party. The unusual thing was, everyone in church was just sitting quietly—no movement, no talking. I found a place to sit and began to hear the voices more clearly.

"Welcome home!"..."We've been waiting for you."..."It's so wonderful to see you and be with you to celebrate!" It appeared that the celebration went beyond the people sitting in the pews. It sounded as if all the angels in Heaven were celebrating. I was so excited and could barely contain myself—it seemed impossible that no one else could hear it—they sat somber, unaffected, and silent. It was not until much later that I realized the full impact of that day when I heard an evangelist say that "there will be much rejoicing and singing of the angels and saints of Heaven over the salvation of one lost sinner." (Luke 15:10)

Lord, You've Got to be Kidding!

I don't know why, but ever since I was born again, I had the crazy notion that I was the only Catholic who ever had this experience. Since I came into a knowledge of spiritual things through reading all those books, and no person I knew had witnessed to me, I had no one to talk to about it. I did know two women who had left the church years before, and I thought that it might have been because they too had met the Lord. I could see that it would have set them apart, and that they would have been misunderstood by others in the church. Maybe they had to leave, and it looked like I would too. I supposed I would just find a Bible-preaching church and join up. I gave a few thoughts to the reaction of my family, and decided to feel my way around. I began dropping lines like, "I think I'll visit other churches. It never hurts to find out what other people believe and what other religions are all about." The reaction was as negative as I suspected it might be, except for Chet who wanted me to "be happy." The same time I was dropping hints to my friends and family, the Lord was busy dropping a few hints of His own. One morning I woke up to a strange thought. It was about volunteering to teach catechism release time for the church. I dismissed it as a silly wake-up thought and pushed it out of my mind, but over the next few days, the idea came back to me, strongly, and over and over. I woke up one night to a voice saying, "Do it now. Volunteer." No matter what I was doing or where I was, or what I was talking about, the words came back. I finally decided that it was the Lord trying to get through to me, and I knew that He would keep it up until I volunteered. *But, Lord,* I thought, *You've got to be kidding. I've only been through the church doors once in a long, long time. I haven't seen the inside of a confessional for over six years, and teach catechism—been there, done that, and not very well. Besides, I should be getting involved in a Bible-preaching church. You are kidding, aren't you Lord?* And the Lord said, "Volunteer." So, sometime early in August, I went to Sunday mass and stopped afterward to see the priest and volunteered. I have completely taken leave of my senses, I thought, but I was filled with a real joy.

I knew that God had forgiven my sins, but after volunteering to teach catechism, I had the feeling that besides going to church on a regular basis, I should go to confession. I read in the church bulletin that confessions were to be held on Thursday at 3:00. I arranged a sitter and drove to town. All the way, I pleaded with God. "Please, God, don't let anyone else be there. I'll die if anyone overhears my confession—and, God, just let it be me and Father Perk—please, not that new foreign priest—I don't understand a word he says." I continued this prayer the nine miles into town. I was relieved when I went into church and no one else was there. It took me about a minute to realize that no priest was there, either. I looked at my watch—3:10—I couldn't have missed it. I turned to walk out and noticed a church bulletin on the floor. I picked it up and read, "Confessions Wednesday, 3:00." *Wednesday! Impossible—I couldn't have made a mistake!* I walked out of church. *Now what?* I decided to go shopping as long as I was in town, but my feet wouldn't move. I tried to move my body to walk around the corner, but I stood glued to the spot like a big idiot! *Now what, Lord?* No answer. *Lord, I know You are there—what should I do?* Still no answer.

"Mary!" The sound of my name startled me. I turned to find a little old lady friend of my grandmother. How she recognized me, I'll never know. It had been many years since I had seen her. After a few friendly exchanges about our families she asked what I was doing there. I told her about the mistake in confession time and she said, "Go to the parish house and ask father to hear your confession." Then she went into the church herself. All of a sudden, I was in the Valley of Decision. Should I just forget the whole thing, or follow her advice? Since her words sounded more like a command than a suggestion, I decided to go for it. I rang the door of the parish house, and Father Perk opened it. Thank God it was him! He led me into his office and I sat down. "Hear your confession? Of course! Go ahead." And he knelt down next to me. *Oh, Lord, You've got to be kidding.* But, He wasn't—He was giving me exactly what I had prayed for all the way into town!

On the way home I reflected on the lessons I learned in that one afternoon. First, God controls all circumstances. Second, often He withdraws His "sense of presence" from us when we have a choice to make. He really lets us exercise our free will. Isn't it wonderful that our Lord isn't pushy or demanding? He knew that I had to do the choosing. He answers prayer in many ways, but in this situation He answered me exactly the way I prayed, which was a great lesson in itself. God has a marvelous sense of humor, and I really knew it that day. I might add that I never went to confession to anyone but the Lord after that, but this was a step in my life I had to take, and the Lord led me all the way.

It looked like, for the time being anyway, I'd remain in the Catholic church. The Lord wasn't in a hurry to hustle me out. In fact, the more I turned things over to Him, the more He confirmed that I was where He wanted me to be. I was content to leave it all in the Lord's hands. The joy and peace I was experiencing was wonderful. I began to spend more time in God's Word and was amazed how clear many things had become. I also began to feel a deep desire to share the Lord with everyone I could, especially those whom I loved most, but as soon as I mentioned anything, I got confused looks. I was beginning to see that sharing what I now knew was not going to be easy. After all, my family knew all about God. They went to church, led good lives, believe in Heaven and Hell, and prayed the rosary. They looked at me and thought that what I was saying and sharing was part of some weird phase I was going through and they were just going to sit back until it passed. I thought of the Scripture in Matthew 10:32: "Whosoever therefore shall confess me before men, him will I confess also before my Father which is in Heaven," and I knew that God wanted me to share my testimony. I needed to trust Him to lead me and to give me the words to say when the time came.

Hello! Are There Any Catholic Christians Out There?

I really wanted to talk to a woman I knew who went to a Bible-based church. I contacted her and told her what had happened to me. She seemed pleased and told me that she had prayed for my family for years. That was the extent of our conversation, and I was so let down. I believed that we would be in the middle of a wonderful discussion about the Lord and when we didn't even talk about Him, I guess I was pretty surprised. All those books that I had read talked about Jesus and the things He was doing in the lives of so many people, and here before me was a born-again Christian of some 25 years, and she had not one thing to say except that she was glad that I was finally saved. She did share several pamphlets with me, all of them talking about the salvation experience.

Only one was different—it told of a man who had been a cardinal in the Catholic church for many years, and when he opened up his heart to Christ he could no longer remain a Catholic because it was a mixed-up church. He strongly advised leaving the church as he did and finding a church that taught about salvation. Needless to say, this little pamphlet caused much turmoil inside of me and I had three of the most sleepless nights of my life. How could the Lord be leading me to stay in a church that was so off the mark? And what about the woman I spoke to? She had been a family friend for over 30 years and had never once mentioned Jesus and what He did for us. (Later, as I began witnessing, I discovered several friends of fifteen and twenty years who were born-again Christians and I had never known!)

I didn't know what to do, so I finally decided that since Jesus had chosen me for His own, that He had a plan for me, He also knew about my concerns and questions—the answers for me were in His hands. I turned all of my feelings over to Him and for the first time in those three nights I felt totally at peace and slept beautifully. This wonderful feeling of peace lasted until the following afternoon. I had an appointment in a nearby city and was on my way there when suddenly I was upset all over again. *Oh, Lord,* I thought, *why did I ever have to be a Catholic in the first place? Why couldn't I have been a Baptist or a Methodist, or something else? Should I be thinking of leaving the church? Was I wrong to get involved with teaching catechism?*

As my mind became more cluttered with thoughts like these, my concentration on driving just about ceased. When I finally realized that I was still behind the wheel, I saw that I had turned down the wrong street and major construction was underway. Workmen, trucks, and equipment were everywhere and I couldn't back up. I pulled into the only empty space I could see to wait until a few of the big machines had moved. I glanced to my left and saw a store across the street named "Adam's Place," a Christian bookstore. I decided to go in and pass the time there instead of sitting in the car trying to avoid stares and getting angry glances from the workmen outside. I looked at shelves of books and could not find a single one by a Catholic. *Great,* I thought, *I should have known better.*

The woman in the store came over and offered assistance and suddenly I was telling her everything. I was really fighting tears and I could tell that she wanted to help me, but apologized when she couldn't. "No, I don't know of a book written by a Catholic who has been born again." She truly looked sorry. I started to leave the store, absolutely crushed, when she came after me. "Just a minute, we just received a new shipment of books and I think one of them had the word Catholic on it." She opened a box and there on the top were not only one, but three books either by Catholic authors or about Catholic experiences. *Hear My Confession* by Father Joseph Orsini, *I Leap for Joy* by Sister Mary Bernard, and *Catholic Pentecostal* by Wead. I bought all three and in the next few days read them all. *So, Lord, I'm not the only flipped-out Catholic, and I am not alone in the church.*

After much prayer, I asked the Lord for guidance as I dealt with things in my life. I even wrote a letter to Father Orsini, but never mailed it. The Lord knew it wouldn't be necessary, for the next day in church I picked up a bulletin that announced a meeting for people interested in a "Life in the Spirit" seminar. I never knew about anything like this, but I had a feeling of peace settle over me and I knew that I was to attend. I must have asked at least 10 people to go with me—three said a reluctant okay, but when the actual day arrived, one by one they canceled out.

When I walked into the meeting room of the church I knew instantly that I was right where God wanted me. I felt peaceful and excited at the same time. I was overjoyed to be there even before the actual meeting began. The speaker was a Catholic priest who gave a terrific testimony of how he met Jesus as his Lord and Savior. He then went on to talk about the Holy Spirit's presence in our lives. As soon as we accept Jesus, the Holy Spirit takes up residence within us. Father explained that we could rely on the guidance and direction of the Holy Spirit, and even experience Him in a deeper way through the Baptism in the Spirit ("When the Holy Spirit who is truth comes, He will guide you into all truth." John 16:13a) I enrolled in the seven-week seminar anxious to learn more about God the Father, Jesus, and the Holy Spirit. I wasn't sure I understood everything about what was called the Holy Spirit Baptism, but I was sure of one thing: I didn't want to miss out on a single thing that God had in store for me.

One afternoon following the meeting, I closed the door in Chet's office and knelt in front of the big chair and prayed. I prayed that the Lord would baptize me in the Holy Spirit. Nothing happened. I didn't know what I expected—maybe I thought that something would fall out of Heaven upon me, or I would have a vision, or at least feel different—but I didn't, I just kept kneeling. How surprised I was when from somewhere deep inside of me came the most beautiful sense of the Holy Spirit's presence. I felt it like water in a spring bubbling up until I couldn't contain the feeling anymore and I opened my mouth to praise God when a language poured out of me that I had never used before. As the language flowed from me, an awareness of being lifted came over me and I felt my spirit rising. I know that my body was still kneeling, but I felt as though I was kneeling above it. The joy and peace and overwhelming love I experienced is beyond description. God had been faithful to answer my prayer. I knew that when I became a Christian that the Holy Spirit took up residence within me, but this was more than His just being there, it was as if He was released in me in a deeper way. This was God's power at work and I knew that God, out of His glorious, unlimited resources had given me the mighty inner strengthening of His

Holy Spirit. Luke 11:13b tells us that God will give the Holy Spirit to those who ask for Him.

In the days following this wonderful experience with the Holy Spirit, my desire to witness was increased along with my desire to read the Word. I had read in a book by Bob Mumford that a spirit-filled believer should be locked up for about six months until they settled down. That was really true in my case. I was so happy and excited in the Lord that I wanted to tell the whole world to sit down while I told them about Jesus. It didn't take me very long to realize that my enthusiasm wasn't being shared, especially with those closest to me, the ones I wanted most to share with—my family. I felt several of them eyeing me with suspicion; one even admitted later that she was sure I had reached the "peak" and they'd be carting me off to a home before long. Everything in the Bible was becoming more meaningful, and I began to see the Word as God's love letter to me. I even began putting my name into some of the passages I read and it became very personal. My relationship with the Lord was growing and was becoming more wonderful each day. It seemed as though time didn't exist when I was praying and reading the Bible. What seemed like minutes was usually an hour or more.

I was tremendously blessed through my association with other Christians I had met during the seminar, and after that ended, I continued to attend prayer meetings. I joined a Bible study and felt very at peace with my new life in Christ. I knew that with each step I was moving into a closer walk with God. However, even though I had contact with many people in the prayer group, I had no special friend or prayer partner who I could share with. I prayed daily that the Lord would give me someone to fill this place. Now I can look back and see the Lord's purpose in not answering my prayer right away. All of my life I have had someone to do things with me. I became used to that and didn't develop the confidence to do things on my own. I relied on my parents and family, roommates, close friends and finally Chet. Everything I did, every place I went was with somebody. The Lord knew that I had a need to be separated, to stand alone, and He provided it for me. The very first decision I made without consulting another person was my decision to invite Christ into my life. It was very apparent to me at that moment that I was alone. I did not have an acquaintance with another person whom I knew had done what I was about to do, outside of the people I had read about and the one person who attended the Bible-preaching church. It seemed that I had no one I could share with, with the exception of the Lord Himself. It was a time of growth for me, and I could almost touch the trust I was gaining in Christ. I don't know the exact date it happened, but the Lord did answer my prayer.

Shirley had been a neighbor for many years, but outside of knowing who she was, I did not have a relationship with her. One day we saw each other and I shared about the prayer meetings I was attending. She expressed a desire to come to one. We started to go together every week and, because it was a 26-mile drive round trip, we had plenty of chances to talk. Before long, we were praying together in the afternoons or over the phone or in whatever situation the Lord provided. And, wonder of wonders—Shirley was a Catholic! She had a different experience than I. She had always been church-minded and involved and had always trusted Jesus. It seemed natural for her to be a part of the prayer meetings and to open up to the Baptism in the Spirit. Being a Christian seemed to have always been a way of life for her and I felt like I was just beginning.

**"Yes, ask anything in My name, and I will do it."
John 14:14**

From the time I began attending prayer meetings, I was impressed at the number of people who shared about a healing they had or that someone close to them had received. I was a little skeptical. I wanted to believe that Jesus was still healing people, but a part of me wasn't quite sure. The Lord worked in me in such a way that it erased forever any doubt I might have about His healing power today.

In 1969 shortly after Tony, our first son, was born, I began to experience stiffness all over my body, especially in the mornings. I pushed it aside as tiredness. Both Chet and I were overwhelmed with the poor sleeping habits of our Tony—our heads hardly hit the pillow and he would be up. It just seemed logical that this tremendous lack of sleep was really getting to us both. That made sense until Chet quit complaining. I was jealous that he was getting more sleep and feeling great, while each day I was more exhausted and hurting harder. It was getting so that even when I did get to bed I would feel a steady, dull ache all over. My fingers were hard to bend and I had to rely on Chet more and more to help me with everything from opening cans to zipping and unbuttoning for me. He urged me to see a doctor, but I insisted I was just tired. The mornings were the worst, and I would have to pull myself up on the bedpost to get up. The thought of my feet hitting the floor panicked me. Finally, one morning, I got out of bed and fell flat on my face. I made an appointment that day.

The doctor I saw did tests and then referred me to a bone specialist who told me that I had symptoms similar to those of rheumatoid arthritis, and even though it did not show up in my blood tests he recommended that I begin a program of taking aspirins. I began with 12 daily and increased it to 16 or more in the weeks to come. A visit to Mayo Clinic confirmed that I did indeed have arthritis, however, not rheumatoid. They worked with me on exercises I could do and advised me to stay on the aspirins. It did give me some relief, but I was never without pain. I took the aspirin faithfully from 1969 until one afternoon in 1975.

I had been asked by a neighbor to decorate a cake for a graduation party and I agreed to do it. The day came to bake the cake, but I woke up with three fingers on my right hand in severe pain. There was no way I could bend them and the pain increased as the morning wore on. I knew I would have to call my neighbor and tell her that she would probably have to buy a cake when I felt the Lord say, "Ask me." I was a little apprehensive—What if I asked God to heal me and He didn't? I was so miserable that I decided that maybe prayer was the best thing I could do. I didn't even know how to ask the Lord. Should I get on my knees? Should I read Scriptures on healing? I decided to just hold my hand up in the air. "Jesus, I've heard a lot about Your healing lately and I believe what the Bible said about all of the healing You performed, but I'm still not sure about You healing today. Is it for me too, Lord? If it is, I want to be healed. Jesus, I ask in Your name that You would heal my fingers and I thank You."

I didn't feel anything but a deep peace. I knew God had heard me. Within minutes my hand felt terrific. Within the hour, the pain in my body diminished considerably too. I felt better than I had for a long, long time and I was able to stop my aspirin program. It was over ten years later before I began to have problems in my body due to the onset of osteo-arthritis, which the Lord dealt with in a number of ways, from medications, surgeries, and yes, even more instant healings. At the same time that the Lord dealt with me physically, He was also working in me spiritually.

"So if the Son sets you free, you will be free indeed"
John 8:36

I had stopped going to mass on Sundays, so praying the rosary began to grow into a real devotion. At first it was my link to the church, but then I began to pray a Novena that lasted 54 days—27 days in petition, and 27 days in thanksgiving. I enjoyed the quiet time saying the rosary provided me, and it was very easy to do. The little booklet I used was beautiful, covering portions of the lives of Jesus and Mary. I continued to pray this way off and on for six years. I made a decision after completing one of the 54-day Novenas: I vowed to Mary that I would say them every day for a solid year. I kept my promise and did just that, never missing a single day. I seldom thought of God or Jesus, but I prayed to Mary. My devotion was strictly to her. 1974 ended and my commitment to pray for a solid year came to a close. It had been such an easy thing to do that I promised Mary that I would say one every day for the rest of my life.

I was a Christian now and had started to read the Bible and learn Scriptures. I prayed and spent time with the Lord each day. Fifteen minutes of that time I prayed my Novena. I became bothered during the Lord's time that I was not spending it all with Him and I started to feel uneasy whenever I began the rosary. It became more and more difficult, but I kept it up anyway. I had two weeks left to finish one 54-day Novena before beginning the next one when a strange thing happened. I started to forget the prayers. I actually had to read the Hail Mary, and the Lord's Prayer from the book. The minute I looked away, I couldn't remember a word or where I was and I would have to start all over. In addition to that, every time I picked up the rosary and my little devotional, I began to feel like a cat on a hot tin roof. I couldn't concentrate or sit still. I started to ask Jesus for help—I felt He wanted me to quit, but I was concerned about breaking a promise I made to Mary. If He made it clear to me that I must stop, I would do it, but if on the last day of the novena, He hadn't said anything, I would begin a new Novena. On the last day, I still wondered what to do.

I began to say the prayers. Immediately when I turned the page in the devotional, the word "LAST" came up off of the page and hovered above the book. At first it startled me, but it was late and I was tired, so I brushed it off. I continued and turned the next page. The word "END" popped up off of the page in the same manner. I turned to the next page and the word "FINISHED" did the same thing. I had been in this same book for six years, I could have just memorized those three places and in my tired state may have just imagined the words lifting off of the page. Then, I closed the booklet and moved my left hand to put the rosary down, but for some reason, I couldn't let it go. In fact, my hand gripped the beads tighter and tighter. I could see my knuckles changing color. My whole focus was on my hand, and it was as if the rest of my surroundings had vanished. That afternoon I purchased a book called *Come Away My Beloved.* I reached for it with my free hand and opened it, and began to read these words:

> "Drop those things which thou graspeth in thy hand and
> place thy hands in mine. Wrest thine eyes from those things
> thou holdest precious. Loose thine affections from all others,
> for so shall thy heart be free to seek me without distraction." [1]

The room was filled with the presence of the Lord. He freed me to love Him, first, above and before anyone else. I have not prayed the rosary since that day. More and more He led me to release "those things I held dear," and He continues to fill me with more and more of Himself. The Lord answered my prayers in many ways—through other people, through the books I read, through His Word, and through the still small voice as He spoke deep in my heart.

> **"Ask and you will be given what you ask for,
> seek and you will find,
> knock and the door will be opened unto you."
> Matthew 7:7**

It amazed me how I could have so many answers to prayer, have my eyes opened to spiritual things, see how the Lord was working in so many people, and still forget that the Lord was with me. I'd have doubts, or try "my way" until I became frustrated, then, I'd resort to prayer as a last effort. God constantly permitted situations to come into my life that taught me the importance of praying and turning things over to Him right away. He was always faithful to answer my prayers and to confirm His truth to me.

One day, my in-laws asked to use our car for a short trip they would be taking. We took their car in exchange. When they returned, they called to tell me to pick up the car. It was a super-hot day and I was glad to be returning their car and getting our air-conditioned one back. I got the boys settled into their seat belts and drove to their home. They had a young niece visiting with them, and when I saw how the boys took to her, I invited her to come home with us for the rest of the day. On the way home, we stopped for groceries. The boys were anxious to get home to play games and read stories with our guest, and the grocery trip made them restless and anxious.

We finally arrived home and I went to open the door but the house key that I always kept on my key ring with my car keys was gone. I found out later that Chet had taken it off and put it on top of the refrigerator when he gave the car keys to his parents. We were locked out, and all of the windows were locked tight as a drum from the inside. I tried everything I could think of to get in but failed. By now, both boys were screaming. Without thinking, I had turned the car off, so my frozen food had begun to melt in the heat. My young guest looked pretty solemn and I could see that she wished she hadn't accepted my invitation. It was still four hours until Chet came home. We lived out in the country and my neighbors were at work. My sister-in-law lived about two and a half miles away and I decided to get her help. I certainly wasn't prepared for her reaction to my situation. She was having problems of her own and made it clear that she didn't have time for us right then, and there was no room in her refrigerator my melting groceries. She did have an old house key and suggested I take it and try it out. Who knows—there might be a shot in the dark that it would work. Home again, but only for more disappointment. The key got stuck half-way into the keyhole and wouldn't budge. I couldn't even wiggle it.

"What now?" asked my young guest. I looked at her and said, "I'm going to do what I should have done right away, I'm going to pray!" If she was unsure that the old key would open the door she was even more skeptical that what I was about to do would help. She just stared at me as I began to pray. "Well, Lord," I prayed, "here I go again. As usual, I tried to do it myself. The boys are crabby, my pot pies are melting, and I just noticed that David's diaper is running over. I need a miracle, Jesus." I turned the door knob, and the door opened. Praise the Lord!

Even when I forget to turn to Him, even when I insist on trying all the angles, He patiently waits until I exhaust my resources and come to Him with my need and He is faithful every time! "You can get anything, anything you ask for in prayer, if you believe." (Matthew 21:22) But why does it take me so long to ask??

God Is Always Full of Surprises

Shirley and I had become good friends by this time, attending prayer meetings, praying together in the afternoons, sharing our new lives with one another. Several other Christians we met invited us to a Friday night prayer meeting at a home near us. Shirley was convinced that the Lord wanted us to accept the invitation. "We need fellowship, they need support, and our going will be a help to both us and them." I agreed to go along with her. We really enjoyed our first visit with the group and began to get more involved with them as the weeks passed. The blessings that Shirley and I received through this prayer fellowship are too many to count, but one special time stands out in my mind.

Since becoming a Christian, I had heard the term "slain in the spirit" a number of times, but did not know much about it beyond the fact that it was a special "touch" from the Lord and those who experienced it felt extremely blessed. One evening at our prayer meeting, we were overwhelmed by the Lord's presence. We were standing in the living room praying when we began to quietly praise the Lord. I felt a light touch on my forehead and opened my eyes to see who had touched me, but there was no one standing near me. Thinking I had imagined it, I closed my eyes and continued to pray. Suddenly, I had the most pleasant feeling. A gentle touch on my forehead and I felt as though I was floating backward. I found myself on the floor smiling and praising the Lord. I never felt more loved and more at peace than at that moment. I had absolutely no doubt that the Lord had touched me. I'm not one to seek experiences, and if anyone had told me that this would happen to me that night, I probably would have stayed at home, but when the Lord is at work He handles all of the circumstances according to each individual's needs. I must say that this didn't happen regularly in our prayer group; in fact, this was the only time I ever attended when we were blessed in this way and it was more than two years later when I experienced being slain in the spirit again.

I learned so many things during this time and Shirley and I were blessed in a multitude of ways through our friendship and prayer time with one another. Although I found it easy to pray with Shirley, I was uncomfortable praying out loud when others were present. I thought my prayers sounded awful while everyone else's sounded so beautiful. The Lord arranged a special experience for me to illustrate how much He wanted me to pray just the way I felt.

One afternoon Shirley and I got together to pray and I began to pray the goofiest prayer ever—I was praying for everything from people in foreign countries to who knows what else. *Good grief,* I thought, *I'd better just be quiet and let Shirley pray before I utter one more foolish word.* I was pretty embarrassed, but so relieved when she didn't comment on my prayer.

The next afternoon when we met to pray, another friend joined us. We really enjoyed her visits and were always delighted to have her pray with us. That afternoon when she began to pray, Shirley and I just stared at her with our eyes wide and our mouths hanging open—she had her eyes closed and her hands lifted and was praying word for word the exact prayer I had prayed the day before. Coming from her it sounded beautiful and sincere.

I knew immediately what the Lord was teaching me through this—I had my focus on myself, how I sounded, and what others would think. I was critical of how I prayed and wanted to impress anyone in earshot, and when I didn't, I was angry that I even opened my mouth. The Lord showed me that day that prayer is from the heart. My prayer was centered around me rather than on God. Prayer isn't meant to entertain or impress those around; rather, it is sharing our feelings and thoughts, and bringing our requests to God alone. That is what made the prayer so beautiful when this lady prayed—the Lord was her total focus.

Happy Birthday!

Isn't Jesus wonderful! I can't wait for each day to begin. Something new and exciting happens all of the time when Jesus is in your life. Even the days that hold disappointments turn out to be special blessings. On October 25, 1975, I had such a day.

It was my birthday, and the day was going to be great—at least that was the attitude I woke up with. It was short-lived, however, when Chet and the boys didn't acknowledge my birthday. Could they have forgotten? As the morning dragged on, it appeared that everyone had forgotten my birthday—even my own mother hadn't called. I had to go to town to run some errands, and I was anxious to get into the car and just drive. I was having a pity party and I didn't want Chet and the boys to see that I was upset and fighting tears.

I knew that Jesus would understand how I felt, and as soon as I got out of sight of the house, I poured out my heart. I figured He would sympathize with me. Instead, in the most gentle voice He said, "Mary, Mary, every year people all over the world forget my birthday." That's all, just those words, but the way they ministered to me was overwhelming. Jesus had permitted this in my life just to reveal to me the indifference of people toward the One who created them, the One who loved them so much that He was born in a stable, became less than the angels, and gave His life for them. How His heart must break as people all over the world turn their backs on Him.

By the time I returned home from my errands I was rejoicing and praising God. It turned out that my birthday wasn't forgotten after all, and Chet and the boys were waiting to surprise me when I came in the door. Mom, my aunts and others called throughout the afternoon and the day truly turned out to be great.

Two months later, I was teaching a religion class and the children were all excited and looking forward to Christmas. I listened to them talking about the presents they were going to get and the company coming or the ski trips and other things they were going to be involved in—all of the worldly things that get our attention. I took the opportunity to share with the class about the true meaning of Christmas. We talked about Jesus and His birth and prayed for a Christmas centered on Him. I know that the Holy Spirit planted the seeds for that teaching on my birthday and it blossomed into one of the most effective classes I ever taught. The lesson I had originally planned to teach was forgotten and I experienced the joy of seeing the Holy Spirit teach. I praise Him that He was able to use me in this way. "Praise the Lord, call upon His name, declare His doings among the people, make mention that His name is exalted." (Isaiah 12:4)

I had not thought about that lesson for a long time, but as we all know, birthdays come, and birthdays go, and the years have a way of passing quickly. I had benefited greatly from the lesson the Lord had taught me but I never dreamed that He would use a similar experience to teach me an even deeper truth. The lesson was brought back to me when I celebrated another birthday five years later.

There was one huge difference this time: only three people, the three people who mattered most—Chet, Tony, and David—had forgotten my birthday. They did not acknowledge it in any way at all, in contrast to every one else! I had phone call after phone call from my aunts and in-laws, my mom and others—always when Chet and the kids were outside, or busy in another part of the house.

Chet's company was having an open house, and the four of us attended that afternoon. To my surprise, one of the secretaries even wished me a happy birthday! Others sitting around her picked up on it and extended good wishes too. Surely, by now, I thought my three men would have caught on, but already a feeling of hurt was growing within me. It was time to leave the open house and I could hardly speak. I was really overwhelmed by the hurt I was feeling. I had no idea that I could ache so badly inside. I tried to put my feelings into perspective, but the hurt seemed to go so deep. I never dreamed that anyone could cause these feelings in me. We were just getting into the car when someone yelled to me to have a happy birthday.

Chet and the boys heard and I could tell by their faces that this was no joke—they had absolutely no idea that it was my birthday. Chet's response was so hard to handle. In all of our years together except on these two birthday occasions, he always had cards, balloons, and gifts.

This time, without even looking at me, he said, "Well, I suppose we might as well go to the mall and get you some kind of gift." That did it. What he said and the tone of his voice ripped through me and the deepest hurt I ever felt surged through my body. I knew if I spoke I'd cry, and Chet and the boys couldn't seem to think of anything to say either. We drove in complete, uncomfortable silence to the mall. They bought me a full length mirror to hang behind the bedroom door. I mumbled a thanks, but I didn't care what the gift was or even if I got one. All I could think of was how cold and unfeeling and insensitive it all was.

When we arrived home, Chet began to put the mirror up right away. I could not believe it. Through all of this, not one of them said happy birthday or showed me any sign of being sorry. The hurt was so strong I could barely stand it. Then Chet looked at me and said, "What in the world does it take to please you—we got you a present, didn't we?" I burst into sobs, tears streaming down my face. Suddenly Chet's face softened and he put his arms around me and held me close. "I am so sorry," he said. I tried to explain that my feelings were so intense that I felt that the Lord was somehow behind everything, but it didn't make much sense.

We got through the rest of the day and I felt very close to Chet because of the way he responded to me when I began to cry. However, I could not set the whole experience aside. My emotions had been so strong. I decided to go for a ride just to get away by myself so I could have some time with the Lord. As soon as I got out of the driveway I began to ask Him: What was wrong, Lord? Why did Chet act like he did, and what about my children? What was wrong with them—why did they do this to me? I turned on the radio, and a song that I had never heard before gave me my answer: "What's wrong with My children, why don't they praise Me? Am I not the King of Kings? Am I not the Lord of Lords? What's wrong with My Children, why don't they praise Me, I've given them everything, yet they have no joy." [2]

My spiritual eyes were opened and I could see why the Lord had permitted me to feel the intense hurt and experience all of the emotions I did that day, and why it had to come through my husband and my children. The first birthday lesson five years ago was to show me the world's indifference to the Lord. This was the indifference of His own—myself included—those who know Him personally as Savior and Lord. I thought of all those times when I knew He was waiting for me but I chose something else to do. All those times I sought advice from others and didn't sit at His feet. All those times when I could have reached out to someone in His name, but I remained silent.

When I returned home, I did spend time in prayer. It had been an overwhelming day, and the lesson I learned needed to be digested in a quiet place. After I prayed, I read a message in *God Calling* called "Deserters":

> "You must believe utterly. My love can bear nothing less. I am so often "wounded in the house of my friends." Do you think the spitting and scorn of my enemies, the mocking and reviling hurt me? No! "They all forsook Him and fled." "I know not the man." These left their scars. So now, it is not the unbelief of my enemies that hurts, but that my friends who love Me and know Me, cannot walk all the way with Me, and doubt My power to do all that I had said. More than the nail piercing in His hands and feet is the heart hurt when His own children ignore Him." [3]

Now Hear This!!

How could I help but share all of the wonderful things the Lord was doing in my life? Well, I couldn't—I had to share and share I did, but the response I had expected wasn't the one I received. The one who heard first-hand all that was going on was Chet. Not an opportunity slipped by that I didn't "share" the things that happened to me. Now, as I look back at that time, I marvel that he didn't lock me up. Between dropping gospel tracts on the floor in front of his desk and leaving the Bible open right under his nose (with Scriptures like "This is the day of salvation" highlighted), to opening up the doors and windows and turning up the volume so every Christian preacher's voice could blast out enabling everyone in earshot to hear, to my continual singing all my favorite Christian selections, to relating in extensive detail all of the miracles of the day...it is a wonder to me how Chet survived it all. Truly, the Lord must have held him up.

Everything was just fantastic in my life. A lovely home, great kids, perfect marriage—how shocked I was when a friend gave me a tape on healing in the marriage and in the home. Of course, I took it just so I wouldn't hurt her feelings, but I certainly had no intention or need to listen to it. A couple of more days and Chet would have heard the gospel according to Mary Ann and finally say the commitment prayer found on the back of the tract on the floor and we would live happily ever after, praising God together into eternity. Shirley must have been thinking along similar lines about her husband, Jim. We were so in love with Jesus that we were certain both Jim and Chet would fall in love with Him very soon, too.

A Full Gospel Businessmen's meeting was being held on a Saturday night and Shirley and I thought it would be great if the four of us went. We talked about it at length, and decided that after hearing the great speaker, Jim and Chet couldn't help but come forward. We even agreed in prayer claiming Matthew 18:19-20: "and, I tell you more, whenever two of you on earth agree about anything you pray for, it will be done for you by My Father in Heaven." We agreed that Jim and Chet would come to the meeting, hear the speaker, and accept Christ. I was so sure that it would all work out in that exact fashion that I went into town and bought Chet a Bible. At the same time I canceled my order for a book called "Unequally Yoked Wives."

Chet and I used to play cards once a month with some very special friends. Actually, we used cards as an excuse to get together. Mostly, we ate and visited and just had a good time. We both looked forward to it, but this Saturday would be different. We would be going to the FGBM meeting. I was so certain that Chet would be all for this plan that I didn't even bring it up until Saturday morning. His reaction just about flattened me! "No!" he shouted, "this Jesus business has gone far enough. You are driving a wedge in our marriage." The outburst was so unlike Chet and the words he used were so out of character for him, I could barely believe it.

I immediately recognized the Lord in this. How could I have been so blind? It all came so clear in that one moment. I was so busy trying to do the Lord's work that I had neglected to let the Lord in on it. Even the prayer Shirley and I agreed upon was part of our great plan. I ran into the small office in the back of the house and knelt down. Jesus is so tender. He forgave me for my foolishness and my selfish ideas and began to teach me where I began to turn my eyes off of Him and onto myself. The first thing I did was listen to the tape I was given. The voice spoke of "driving a wedge" into a marriage, a confirmation that the Lord had spoken to me through my husband. Later, when I mentioned "driving a wedge" in our marriage to Chet, he had absolutely no recollection of ever saying it to me. We went out that night to spend time with our friends and the blessed assurance that I was in God's will stayed with me all evening, and I felt closer to the Lord and to Chet than before. Incidentally, Jim never went to the meeting with Shirley and I'm sure the Lord revealed many things to her through the experience.

One thing I was sure of—God knew our heart's desire. He heard our prayers for our husbands, and I knew in His good time, they would know Him.

Oh, No—Not Me, Lord!

Shirley and I met one afternoon for prayer. She was particularly burdened by a need in her parish. The church council was looking for a secretary and the search was becoming very frustrating—no one was interested or available. We prayed that day, and for three weeks afterward, but there was still no sign of a secretary.

Shirley and I attended church in the same city, but we went to different parishes. Every so often, I would go to her church on a Saturday evening because the services were at a perfect hour and very convenient when I knew I would be unable to make a Sunday service at my church. It was on such a Saturday when I entered Shirley's church. I was a little late, and the church was full, but I managed to squeeze into the back row. I could see Shirley sitting up in the front and hoped I would have a chance to say "hi" after the service.

During the sermon, the priest took time to mention the need for a church secretary. He came down into the aisle, looked around at everyone and pleaded for a volunteer. As soon as he asked for a volunteer I heard a clear voice behind me say, "Mary Ann, you do this!" There was no one behind the back row, so I didn't bother to turn around— I knew it was the Lord, and I also knew that He had spoken to Shirley about me doing this at the same time.

When the service ended, Shirley spotted me and made a beeline for the back of the church. She couldn't wait to tell me what the Lord wanted me to do. I told Shirley that there was no way I could be anyone's secretary—I not only didn't know a thing about it, but I didn't even go to her church. Shirley urged me to pray about it, and she then told me that it wasn't for her parish, but for the diocesan council in the Duluth diocese. Now I was certain that I didn't want to get involved. I told Shirley that I would pray, but I didn't. I knew what the answer would be and I didn't want to hear it. The Lord remained quiet about the matter for a couple of days. *Good,* I thought.

Tuesday morning started out on a fairly normal note. I did my regular chores then sat down for a time of prayer. I decided to read through the gospel of Luke and I opened my Bible to that part of Scripture. My reading was going alone quite nicely when I came to Luke 6:46: "You call me Lord, Lord. Then, why don't you obey Me?" The verse seemed to actually have a volume to it. I decided immediately that I had read enough in the Bible for one morning and reached instead for a small packet of Scripture cards that I had recently purchased. It seemed like a great alternative to continuing in Luke, so I pulled out a card...Luke 6:46.

It is so amazing to me that I can be so stubborn. The Lord was speaking to me clearly, but it didn't line up with what I wanted, so I chose again to ignore it. About 1:00 in the afternoon I had a strong feeling to call Shirley. I knew she would be at work and I never called her at work, however, the feeling became stronger, and I had to call. As soon as I heard her voice I felt foolish. "It's me," I said, "And don't ask me why I'm calling. I don't know." "I do," she responded. "I prayed this morning about you and the council work and asked the Lord to have you call me at exactly 1:00 if He wanted you to do this." "Oh, no," I said. Can you believe I was still fighting? I can't type very well and I don't know a thing about secretarial work; I would never be able to handle this responsibility. Shirley, however, disagreed and told me to keep praying. This time, I did pray for the better part of the afternoon. I was accustomed to listening to WWJC, a Christian radio station that went off the air at about 4:45 in the afternoon. After I finished praying and began to start planning supper, I turned on the radio. It was only a short time before the station would be done, but I turned it on anyway—just in time to hear the speaker say, "Today, before we close, I have a special message for you from my wife." She came on and said that we should be excited for new experiences; we shouldn't look backward, but look ahead. Be willing to accept the challenges and move onward and upward.

Later that evening, when the boys were in bed and all was quiet, I sat down to read. I had received some books several weeks earlier and had not had the time to take them out of the package until now. I pulled one out that was on joy in keeping God's commands. It was filled with verses from the Living Bible like James 2:14: "Dear brothers, what's the use of saying that you have faith and are Christians if you aren't proving it by helping others?" and Romans 12:13a: "When God's children are in need, you be the one to help them out."

"I'll do it, Lord, please forgive me for my stubborn disobedience. I want to follow You. I'll go to the council meeting and volunteer to do the secretarial work and what ever else You would have me do."

Once I got into the secretarial position on the council, I decided that I needed a new typewriter. My old typewriter was in poor condition and I knew it wouldn't be up to the task. I shopped around, but the prices were out of my budget. I took the matter to the Lord and He impressed upon me to get the old one repaired. I even got the feeling that He was telling me that it would cost $15.00. I called several places but to just have it cleaned and looked at the cheapest quote I got was $45.00. Chet remembered that an uncle often repaired typewriters, so I gave him a call. He said that he would do it for $25.00. This was the least expensive quote I'd gotten, so I agreed to have him do it. In about 10 days he called me to say that he had the typewriter all cleaned, repaired, and ready to be picked up. When he handed me the bill I saw once again how much the Lord cares about everything concerning us and can handle every situation that touches our lives. The bill read as follows:

```
 $25.00
 -10.00 less relative discount
 $15.00
```

The work on the council turned out to be a rewarding experience. The Lord blessed me in many ways. He did the organizing and the typing, and He even gave me an opportunity to give my testimony to the council before I completed my time with them. Every area where I was weak, uninformed, and inexperienced, He was strong, knowledgeable, and able to do all things.

"With men it is impossible, but not with God: for with God, all things are possible." Mark 10:27

From Lagging Behind to Running Ahead

You probably have gotten the idea by now that I am the greatest foot-dragger of all time, and I have to agree—but I am also the greatest at running out ahead of the Lord, believing that I am in His will without actually taking time to see what He wants.

I had two lovely Christian friends in my life. I wanted so much to share all of the things that the Lord was doing with me. I not only wanted to share my experiences with them, I wanted them to have my experiences, especially where the baptism in the Holy Spirit was concerned. One day, I made the decision to grab my Bible and some tapes on the baptism and surprise them with a visit. I was just running out the door when the phone rang. It was a dear friend that I hadn't seen for quite some time. I told her that I was in a hurry and was sorry that I couldn't talk to her just then, but that I would call her as soon as I had the time. She told me that she would only keep me a minute. She had been praying and the Lord moved her to call me and give me a Scripture verse. The Scripture was Matthew 14-16. I glanced at it but really didn't take the time to focus on it and think about the reason the Lord wanted me to see it.

I met with my two friends and we had a terrific time. We prayed and shared Scriptures and the tapes I brought, and I was able to answer their questions and tell them about my personal experience. My prayer group was having a seminar and I invited them to come. I was thrilled that they were able to come for the first meeting, but the meeting turned out exactly opposite of what I had expected. My friends told me that they were very moved by the love in the group, but didn't feel that the Holy Spirit was at work at all. The person who introduced the topics for the seminar didn't even have a Bible with him and they were not able to get answers to a single question they asked. They told me I would be foolish to continue to attend. I was not going to give up so easily and told them to give it one more chance. I had heard the speaker who was scheduled for the following week, and he was right on target with the salvation message and God's desire to have a deeper relationship with us. I just knew if they came they would have a change of heart. They reluctantly agreed.

My friends had expressed their disappointment with the first night of the seminar, but their reaction to the second meeting displayed even greater disappointment. In fact, I had watched their faces as they listened to the speaker and I could tell they did not like it one bit. They were used to hearing a salvation message, and preaching from the Scriptures, and it was obvious that they weren't hearing it that night. I couldn't believe it either—comparing the first time I had heard the speaker to the way he was speaking at this meeting, well, it was like listening to two different people. He was going on and on about everything totally unrelated to anything I had expected. He never did get the message out, and salvation, the Holy Spirit Baptism, and a relationship with Christ never even entered the talk. I was so critical of him—good grief, even I could have done a better job. Certainly I could have explained things a lot clearer and brought up things that mattered instead of all of this grassroots gobbledygook that he was spouting. I knew I was being severely critical, and when everyone broke up into small discussion groups I went into the restroom to pray.

I took some time to examine my feelings and bring them before the Lord. I confessed my critical spirit and asked God to forgive me for being so hard on the speaker. Deep in my heart I still felt angry, but I managed to push that feeling down. When I came out of the restroom, there were my two friends discussing everything I had been thinking. Well, I joined right in—criticism, judgment, a fast tongue, you couldn't hold me down! Needless to say, my friends expressed their disappointment in everything, including me, for being so naive that I would attend such a waste-of-time meeting.

After I left them, I began to drive home and I started to explain my feelings to the Lord. He really let me hear myself and when the realization of what I had said and done hit me, I saw my sin and I knew beyond a doubt that I had been very wrong. The more I tried to justify what I had said, the more the Lord convicted me. I was in tears by this time, and it wasn't because my friends weren't open to what was going on, it wasn't because of the speaker, it was because I had sinned and I would not be at peace until I got right with God.

Upon arriving home, I went directly to a quiet spot and began to pray. "Please, Lord, show me in Your Word something that would shed light on all of this." The verses that came to my mind were in Job 40:1-3. "Do you still want to argue with the Almighty or will you yield? Do you, God's critic have all the answers?" I was without a reply; I felt awful. I put my hand over my mouth and continued to read verse 4. Job's response was also mine: "I am nothing, how could I ever find the answers. I lay my hand upon my mouth in silence, I have said too much already." I knew the Lord was angry with me and I asked if He was also angry with my two friends. I turned the page and my eyes fell on Job 42:7: "I am angry with you and your two friends for you have not been right in what you have said." Then I read Job 42:36: "I was talking about things I knew nothing about and did not understand, things far too wonderful for me." I knew that I had done exactly that and I wept before the Lord and repented of my sin. He forgave me and I felt my joy and peace return.

The Lord led me through Scriptures all throughout the week and revealed that the Scripture references the speaker had used were right on. I learned later that a number of people who had attended the seminar that night had received Christ into their lives as their Lord and Savior. Jesus showed me that my eyes were not on Him but rather on my friends and their reaction. I was so concerned about what I was doing in their lives that I had forgotten about what God was doing. My focus was misplaced and it led to sin. It happens every time we get our eyes off of Jesus and onto ourselves. God also reminded me of the hurried, frenzied way I ran off to speak to my friends that very first time. He is a gentle, loving Savior, not demanding or pushy, and I should have been in a prayerful attitude, waiting on God to act rather than running out ahead of Him and taking matters into my own hands. I realized too, how little I had prayed during this time and how I had neglected fellowship with the Lord—a disaster for any Christian!

I asked the Lord why He had permitted me to go through this terrible situation without stopping me or at least giving me a warning.

He reminded me of the phone call I was in too much of a hurry to pay attention to. I remembered the Scripture verse I was given at that time and I finally took a moment to look it up and read it. "They hear, but don't understand; they look, but don't see! For their hearts are heavy and their ears are dull, and they have closed their eyes so they won't see and hear and understand and turn to God again to let Me heal them." (Matthew 13:14-16)

I finally saw that the Lord did try to let me know that I shouldn't pursue this, for it would surely fail, but I didn't take the time to listen or pray, and everything that happened was brought on by myself. I prayed that God would give me the wisdom to trust Him and to include Him in everything concerning me.

A Lying Tongue

"Keep your tongue from evil, and your lips from speaking lies." Psalm 34:13

One of my heart's desires was to witness to a neighbor of mine. I knew that she did not understand what had happened to me and, more and more, I felt a division in our relationship. We had been so close for many years and suddenly we were unable to share our feelings. I really wanted to, but, for some reason, I didn't know how to bring it up. I did decide that I would focus on praying for her and for a mending of our friendship.

The Lord began to lead me to several Christians who lived near me and between visits with them, prayer, meetings, and my regular Bible study, I became quite busy. I even attended several prayer coffees that were held prior to a John Westley White Crusade. White was an associate of Billy Graham and he was coming to our area to conduct a crusade. I took the Christian Witnessing classes they offered and began to council young people. It was a rewarding experience and it was great to be a part of what the Lord was doing. All of my activities kept me moving further away from contact with my neighbor.

Because of my involvement with the crusade, my attendance in both the Catholic and Lutheran prayer groups, and my new-found interest in talking about Jesus, my neighbor became increasingly curious and confused about me and what I was into. I became aware of this one afternoon when I was teaching catechism. I came out of my classroom just in time to see my neighbor. I went over to say hello, but she turned around and asked if I would please leave so she could speak to the nun in charge. I immediately had a funny feeling come over me accompanied by a sense that this was about me. I had bad feelings for quite some time because of the rift between us, and I didn't know what to do about it. One thing that I had done had been very wrong and I regretted it and felt guilty but didn't know how to fix it.

I wanted so badly to tell my neighbor about Jesus and what He meant to me, and to restore our relationship and include her in my life again, but nothing seemed to work out. One day when I saw her, I could see in her face that she was genuinely hurt by my involvement with all my new friends and activities. Without thinking, I told her that I had called her to come over for coffee the day before, but there was no answer. As soon as I said it, I wanted to run and hide—it was a lie! The words were out of my mouth before I gave a thought to what I was doing. I knew if I tried to confess and explain myself, I would only make matters worse. I didn't say a thing and when we each went our own way, I took it to the Lord. I asked for His forgiveness for the lie I told. I knew I needed her forgiveness too, but I had no clue about how to handle it. I prayed and as I prayed the Lord revealed to me that she had been home and knew I hadn't called her. She knew I had lied and I know that her hurt was only made greater. I couldn't believe how foolish I had been; it made me see how weak I was, and how on guard I had to be against attacks from the devil. I needed to walk so close to Jesus that I wouldn't be caught in traps like lying. I knew I was forgiven, and I also knew that the Lord would arrange a time when things could be set right.

After catechism class, I had an opportunity to speak to the Sister in charge. I found out from her that my neighbor did indeed want to discuss me. She knew I belonged to a Charismatic group and she had spoken to her parish priest about it. He advised her to stay away from me, that the Charismatic movement was not of God. In addition, if I was occasionally attending meetings at the Lutheran church, I must be involved in something wrong. She apparently had spoken to others about me (people I didn't even know) and was advised to speak to someone about getting me out of the release time program. She even told Sister that I could be involved in some kind of plot to overthrow the Lutheran church and that several people had left the Lutheran church already because of the talk of a Holy Spirit Baptism.

I was stunned to discover the extent to which this had progressed. My neighbor's concept of what I was doing went beyond anything I could have dreamed up, and in addition to all of that, she knew that I was a confirmed liar. I shared about my lying and also my about inability to think of a way to make amends. Sister and I agreed to pray about it, believing that the answer would have to come from the Lord and that nothing short of divine interference would make things right again.

Sister and I prayed daily for over a week. One evening, just before I was to leave for a prayer meeting, the Lord impressed upon me that now was the time to go to my neighbor and ask her forgiveness. Because I had only an hour before my sitter arrived, I decided there was no time to see her, so I called. The line was busy, and when I prayed about it, I had a strong feeling that a phone call wouldn't do—I needed to go to her house, and I had to do it right away. I asked the Lord to make a way—the sitter wasn't due for an hour, and Chet wouldn't be home until late that night. I couldn't leave the boys alone, and I knew I couldn't take them with me. I looked at the clock and saw that I had already wasted almost half an hour dragging my feet.

I glanced out of the window and saw Chet drive into the driveway. "Now, get going," the Lord said. I ran out of the house, explaining briefly to Chet as I ran by him in the driveway. I knew that if the Lord brought him home four hours early that He would give me the words to say too. A calm feeling settled over me and I felt a peace inside. I knocked on the door and went in—I could almost feel the Lord standing by me. My neighbor just looked at me with a surprised look. I began to explain why I had come. I confessed my lie and told her how sorry I was. I asked her forgiveness and she reached for me. Before I knew it, we were both crying and hugging and telling each other how much we cared and how much we had missed each other. I felt that a million-pound weight had been lifted from me, and I felt sure she did too. We both knew that we couldn't go back to the way things were, but we knew that there had been a healing in our relationship and we were willing to begin there. Without Jesus, this never could have happened. I had anger too, and felt mistreated. At one point, I would have liked to just forget everything and walk away, but I knew that the Holy Spirit would not allow that.

How good it is to confess our sins before the Lord and experience His forgiveness. How good it is to know that when things are turned over to Him they are taken care of. I learned many things from the Lord through all of this and I felt a little stronger and wiser. I saw the damage the tongue could do, and I knew that I had to be on guard to control it.

"And all things are of God, who hath reconciled us to Himself by Jesus Christ, and hath given to us the ministry of reconciliation" 2 Corinthians 5:18

"I pray that you will begin to understand how incredibly great His power is to help those who believe in Him." Ephesians 1:19

"Blessed is the man whom God corrects..."
Job 5:17

A few weeks after my reconciliation with my neighbor, I was in attendance at a prayer meeting. One of the men there began to share about a problem he was having with his neighbor. The situation was so like the one I had just experienced, I felt led to share with him and the others present. I told them about the broken relationship, the misunderstanding and accusation, and the lie. I then said that one of my reactions was just to forget it and tell her "up your nose with a rubber hose" (an expression used quite often at that time on a popular television series). I told them that after I had prayed and confessed my sin before the Lord, He gave me His perspective and softened my heart, giving me the desire to mend fences. He then provided me the opportunity to restore our relationship.

Several days later, I was reading a book called *The Last Chapter* by A.W. Rasmussen. I was especially impressed by chapter 10, "Removing Spots and Wrinkles." The author refers to Ephesians 5:25-27. He explained that the "spots" are people who have fallen into sin. They have to be "washed out." It's the application of the Word of God which results in the washing process. In many cases, it is a painful and difficult experience. Washing always produces wrinkles—sometimes feelings are hurt and hearts are broken. Only the Holy Spirit can press out the wrinkles. [4]

The things that I read in that chapter kept going over and over in my mind. That evening when I was praying, I picked up a devotional and the message for that day was Ephesians 5:25-33. After reading the message, I opened another book called "Living Light." [5] There was reference in that reading to Ephesians 5. I prayed earnestly that the Holy Spirit would reveal to me anything in my life that would cause a spot or blemish to appear. After praying, I read James 3:5-6: "So, also, the tongue is a small thing, but what enormous damage it can do. A great forest can be set on fire by one tiny spark. And the tongue is a flame of fire. It is full of wickedness, and poisons every part of the body."

The Holy Spirit brought to my mind the prayer meetings I had attended. when He began to speak to me about the sharing that I had done, I wrote down what He said to me:

> "My child, lately you have chosen figures of speech that are unbecoming to one of my children. Just because these sayings are used openly does not make them acceptable. Their use causes a shadow to fall on the whole community even though they are accepted by the world and thought of as mild, unharmful expressions. They cause eyebrows to raise where my children gather."

I recalled then, that as I used the expression the Lord was referring to, I believed I saw the eyebrows of the pastor shoot clean up to his hairline. I dismissed it as a trick my eyes were playing on me but, when the Lord reminded me of it, I realized that the pastor had been shocked by my choice of words—I am sure he recognized it as having a double, or hidden meaning. I asked the Lord's forgiveness, and knew that I received it.

I praise God for the lessons I am learning. I thank Him for His gentleness and patience in dealing with me. No matter how soiled I am, Jesus can wash me white as snow and cleanse my sin. No matter how many wrinkles I have, the Holy Spirit can iron me as smooth as silk. Proverbs 10 tells us that "Anyone willing to be corrected is on the pathway to Life. Anyone refusing has lost his chance."

> "My son, despise not the chastening of the Lord, nor faint when rebuked of Him. For whom the Lord loveth He chasteneth, and encourageth every son whom He receiveth. If ye endure chastening, God dealeth with you as with sons; for what son is he whom the Father chasteneth not? Now no chastening for the present seemeth to be joyous, but grievous: nevertheless, afterward it yieldeth the peaceable fruit of righteousness unto them which are exercised thereby." Hebrews 12:5-11

When I know that all is right between the Lord and me, I am so aware of His closeness. I know that I never want any barriers between us, but rather a clean channel—but oh, so often, things crowd into our lives and we lose our focus. Maybe it comes in the form of doubting, or anger, maybe worry or indifference. Whatever the case, it is important to recognize it and come to the Lord with it. With me, it is a daily thing. I know that I have salvation, and that I am a child of God, but I also know that I have the freedom of choice and sometimes the choices I made— like telling the lie to my neighbor, or using inappropriate expressions— led into sin. I need to seek God's forgiveness and cleansing. I also have learned that when I feel that "all is well," I have a tendency to forget how careful and on guard I need to be. Our adversary is ever watching for an opportunity to rob our joy and lead us into temptation.

> **"Trust in the Lord with all your heart,**
> **and lean not on your own understanding;**
> **In all your ways acknowledge Him,**
> **and He will direct your paths."**
> **Proverbs 3:5-6**

It was a wonderful day in March, 1976. I had spent time with the Lord and I felt so at peace. I had things to do, but each task was easy, and my burdens were light. I didn't think that anything could disrupt the joy I felt. It is amazing how we can feel so lifted to mountain heights one minute and be in the valley the next, but that is exactly what transpired.

Chet surprised me by coming home early from work. We began talking and sharing our day and setting up our plans for the upcoming weekend. Chet shared that he felt something "in the wind" at work, but he couldn't put his finger on it. He didn't know what they had up their sleeve—maybe a paycut, maybe a transfer, maybe even a layoff—who could know? Or, maybe it was nothing at all and he was just speculating because of some things he overheard out of context. Actually, Chet didn't seem to be upset or overly concerned about it, so I decided to just dismiss it and wait until we had more information.

My peaceful attitude and calm lasted until we were in bed. He was already asleep, but my thoughts began racing wildly and I started to react to the things Chet had said as though they were facts. What if the company did something that would change our lives? What if they laid Chet off, or even fired him? What would we do? We were working on the house; we had financial commitments. Oh, my Lord, what if it was a transfer? I was on the church council—what about that? Besides, our families would flip...how could we leave them and our new house? None of this could be God's plan for us. I tried to turn all of these thoughts over to the Lord, but I was so worked up inside that I couldn't pray. I fought with these feelings for three days and nights. On the fourth night, I was alone. Chet had a late appointment and wouldn't be home until after midnight. I put the boys to bed and sat down to talk to the Lord. I could not deal with one more sleepless night and I was determined to spend as much time as I could praying and seeking the Lord in all of this.

I prayed for a very long time. I really wanted God's perfect will for my life, but I also wanted things to go the way I imagined would be the perfect way for us. During my prayer time, the Lord impressed me to read Ruth 1:1-5, and to substitute our names into the situation. This is how it read with the changes I made:

> "Long ago when judges ruled in Israel, a man named Chet from Cherry left the country and moved to a different land. With him were his wife, Mary Ann, and his two sons, Tony and David. During the time of their residence in the new land, Chet died and Mary Ann was left alone with her two sons."

At first, I thought this would be great—putting our names into Scripture—but as I read the verses, I could see this was no game the Lord was playing. For a few minutes, I experienced a heavy, dismal feeling and then I remembered that above all else, I wanted God's will, not mine. "Forgive me, Lord, for doubting Your love."

I reflected on what Jesus had done for me on the cross, and how He had led me to this point in my life. All of the lessons and answers to prayer reminded me how much He cared for every detail concerning us. I knew He would never abandon me or my family, and I was sure He would carry us through whatever was ahead.

I wanted God's will, but if that were a layoff, or a transfer to "a faraway land," then that is what I wanted. If what I had read in Ruth after I substituted our names was to come to pass, I knew that God would take care of that too. After I told Him these things, I was flooded with a warm feeling. It was like a bottle of "liquid love" was being poured over me and the peace of God overwhelmed me. For the first time, I slept peacefully all through the night.

I knew that Jesus wanted to be first in my life, and all I had just experienced had helped me to turn my focus onto Him.

Several months passed and things seemed to settle down to the normal routine. Nothing was mentioned about changes in Chet's work situation and I was sure it had all been his imagination. I did remember the lesson I learned and I continued to set aside a time every day to pray and read the Word. I wanted to keep my focus on Jesus, but somehow, I managed to continue to keep hold of an area that I thought I could handle by myself. I was still preaching to Chet whenever I had an opportunity, and dropping gospel tracts in his path had become a habit. I thought I was handling everything very well until I had a dream that rearranged my thinking on the matter.

In my dream, Chet told me that he had to make a trip to Grand Rapids to pick up a truck. He never returned from the trip, and news came that on the way home there had been an accident and he was killed. I was suddenly surrounded by consoling relatives, but I said nothing. I walked by them and went into an empty room. "Now what, Lord?" I said. Suddenly the room became brighter and a voice spoke to us: "If you will trust My Son in this, You will see a miracle." I left the room and joined the others, informing them that they needn't worry—Jesus would take care of me and the boys. Suddenly, the dream shifted to a school. I took the boys in and Chet was there waiting for us. We played basketball and had a great time. I woke up at this point and thought through the dream. First Chet was dead, and then he was alive. It was like a born-again dream—we are lost and dead in our sin before we accept Christ as our Savior, and when we do, we are alive. After reflecting on the dream, I went back to sleep and slept through the rest of the night.

The following morning, we woke up to a ringing phone. It was someone from Chet's work informing him that he had to go to Grand Rapids to meet with a customer. Chet got his things together and said that he would be home by 5:30 in time for supper. That evening, I had a meal ready by 5:30. I fed the boys at 6:30. By 7:30 I decided I might as well eat something. I wrapped the leftovers in foil for Chet thinking that he would come through the door any minute. By the time I put the boys to bed, the dream I had the night before began to make a trip to the forefront of my mind. I tried to stop thinking about it, but by 10:00 when I sat down to pray, it really took hold of me. That worried, panicky feeling came into my stomach and I began to tell the Lord why Chet had to come home. The boys were so small and the house was a big commitment and I needed him, and on and on, when suddenly I realized what I was doing. "Oh, Lord, please forgive me—I did it again. I took my eyes off of You and allowed Satan's tools of fear and worry to cloud my vision. Lord, I don't know what Your plan for Chet is, but I want Your will, not mine. I know that You will be with me and strengthen me, no matter what. I love You, Lord."

> "Don't be anxious about anything, but in everything, by prayer and petition, with thanksgiving, present your requests to God. And the peace of God, which transcends all understanding will guard your hearts and minds in Christ Jesus." Philippians 4:6-7

As I continued to pray, I felt a slight pressure in my chest that I often had during my prayer time. This time, however, it began to increase until I began to feel waves of that "liquid love" pouring over me just as I had experienced back in March. I was pinned back in the chair, couldn't life my head or arms, and didn't want to. I wanted that feeling to last forever. I was enveloped in the deepest sense of God's presence and His love surrounded me and filled me in a way that I cannot describe. All I could do was say the words, "I love You, Jesus," over and over again. Tears of happiness streamed down my face—they seemed to flow from someplace deep within me and I knew I was in the presence of the Lord. Chet did not come home until 1:00 in the morning, but I knew that the peace I had would have kept me forever, even if he had not returned.

The next morning as I prayed, I felt the Lord asking me if I understood what I had done the night before. I really didn't, but as I waited on Him, I knew that for the first time, I had totally relinquished Chet into His hands, leaving Him free to work in Chet's life. I keep falling in love with Jesus, and this experience made me see that the love I feel is getting stronger and deeper even though it is only a shadow of His love for me. By the way, I never dropped gospel tracks on the floor or left the Bible open to highlighted Scriptures again. Instead, I placed my trust in God to work in Chet's life.

> "Blessed is the man who makes the Lord his trust."
> Psalm 40:4

A Time of Changes

"And we know that in all things
God works for the good of those who love Him,
who have been called according to His purpose."
Romans 8:28

Every month or so, Chet's company had sales meetings in Minneapolis. I was never anxious for him to be gone, but with the Lord, I was at peace about it. The day he left, I was busy with cleaning and laundry. I wanted to get everything done early in the day so I could go into town for groceries. While I was shopping, I walked past a display of books and spotted one called *God's Chosen Fast*. I decided to purchase the book, knowing that I would have plenty of time to read it, since Chet would be in Minneapolis overnight.

The book I bought wasn't very big and it didn't take long to get through the first part of it. I came to the bottom of a page and turned to the next, to see the word "Brainerd" jump out at me. The word looked huge and it was as if no other words were on the page. Along with this came the immediate thought that we would be moving to Brainerd. When I got my bearings, I took another look at the page, to find the sentence with that particular word in it. One of the sentences contained a reference to a book by a man named David Brainerd. I had no doubt that the Lord was using this experience to reveal part of His plan to me. I didn't have any idea how all of this would take place, but I knew that it would in His good time.

About two hours later, Chet called to say good night and to fill me in on his day. "You'll never believe what happened at the meeting. They are realigning the sales territories and there's been a change in mine—they want me to work out of Minneapolis!" My heart just about stopped! "We cannot move to Minneapolis," I said. "No," Chet replied, "I'll just be working out of Minneapolis; they are transferring me to Brainerd." "Praise the Lord," I shouted and Chet said, "What?" "Nothing," I answered, "we'll talk about it when you get home."

I did not know it at the time, but Chet's biggest fear was what my reaction would be. He imagined that I would carry on and rant and rave as I clung to my beautiful trees and patted the siding on the house. He was in for a surprise when he came home to find me checking on Realtors. I was absolutely certain that this was God's plan, and I was excited to see how He would work it all out. Incidentally, the experience I had with the Scripture in Ruth did come back into my thoughts, but God showed me a number of verses that put my mind at ease. Any thread of concern was removed and I felt confident that God would protect us and walk with us every step of the way.

Oh, the Sweet Taste of Pride!

The Lord continually confirmed in some way that this move was His will for us. As we began to get the house ready to be put up for sale, the Lord impressed upon me that when we moved, we were to take only our belongings—anything we had put into the house was to stay. I was fine with that except for one thing.

When Chet and I had picked out our light fixtures for the house, I fell in love with a particular Strauss crystal chandelier. It was beautiful and dainty, a perfect choice for the master bedroom. Unfortunately it was expensive. We had finished choosing all of the other lights we needed, but while we shopped, I kept coming back to that chandelier. At one point, I saw Chet talking to the owner of the store. I saw him smile and the owner nod. He said we could have the light for a few dollars over his cost—still four times higher than we had in our budget. Chet said he wanted me to have the light and would get it for me as a gift from him. The light became even more special after that. I loved how it looked in the bedroom. The boys and I would move the light slightly and shine a flashlight on it, and the crystal prisms would make the walls in the room dance with tiny rainbows.

When the Lord said to leave everything that was part of the house, I couldn't imagine that he meant my light as well. Suddenly keeping that light became a top priority to me—after all, it was more than just a light; it was a special gift. I began to develop an unhealthy desire to keep the light and thought of how I could manage to do that. I decided that if I could get Chet to let me keep it, I could do it in submissiveness to him (isn't that scriptural?).

Chet said that taking the light down would be fine, but I had to get it down before the house was appraised. That meant I had just two days to find a replacement and have it installed. My very first thought after Chet said I could take the light was that I would also take the light from the dining room and the one in the foyer. After all, I liked them too and they would be perfect in the new house. (Ever notice when we begin to follow the flesh and listen to the devil's deception, we can get off course very quickly?)

I didn't take time to pray about any of this; deep down, I knew what the Lord had already said, but I pushed that out of my mind. If I had prayed, I probably would have run across a Scripture like this one: "We justify ourselves in the eyes of men, but God knows our hearts. What is highly valued among men is detestable in God's sight." (Luke 16:15) Maybe recognizing my greed, pride, and rebellion would have hit home and I would have been obedient, but I was too far into myself at this point and I chose instead to get out to the car and race to the nearest lighting store.

I had a 14-mile drive ahead of me and I barely got halfway into the trip when I started to think of what the Lord had said. I hoped that He would let me keep the light. Suddenly, I just spoke out loud, "Lord, is this all right with You? May I take the light or is this my pride and stubbornness getting in the way of Your will?" I no sooner spoke when I rounded a curve in the road and came face to face with a large billboard that some workmen were just finishing putting up. It was a billboard for Crystal Sugar and in big bold black letters I read the words: OH THE SWEET TASTE OF PRIDE!

After reading the message on the billboard, my eyes were opened and I saw clearly what I was doing. I turned around and headed home, on the way confessing my sin before the Lord and praying for forgiveness. I knew that He forgave me, and the desire for that chandelier and the other two fixtures left me for good.

Before we moved to Brainerd, we had to pick out the fixtures for the new house. They were to be delivered to the builders for installation. When we moved in, the house was completely finished top to bottom, even the driveway and landscaping were done. Everything was taken care of, except for one thing. I walked into the master bedroom and there hanging from the ceiling was a 60 watt light bulb. The light we had picked out was never delivered with the other lights, so the contractor just left the bulb there. I kept it like that the entire time we lived in that house, and believe it or not, that 60 watt bulb was more beautiful and special to me than 50 Strauss crystal chandeliers could ever have been!

We are always confronted with choices, and the worldly pleasures have a strong pull. It isn't easy to turn from them, but the Lord will always give us guidance and strength. Trusting in ourselves is foolish, but being obedient and trusting in the Lord is wisdom. (Proverbs 28:26) He commands us to love Him and walk in His ways; to keep His commandments, decrees, and laws. When we do what is right in the Lord's sight, we will be blessed.

"I will instruct you and teach you in the way you should go"
Psalm 32:8a

On August 26, 1976, the doors on the moving van were closed. We waved to the drivers as they pulled out of the yard. The house was empty, and Chet and I took a final walk from room to room. It seemed a little strange—our plan when we built the house was to live in it until the boys were grown and we were retired. Here it was, only two and a half years later and we were moving out.

I picked up my purse and my Bible and a copy of *Come Away My Beloved* and stepped out of the door in front of Chet. He turned to lock the house, and said, "Come on, let's get going." Then, almost as an afterthought, he added, "Go ahead, open one of those books and see what God is telling you now." I didn't expect anything, but I opened *Come Away My Beloved* and read the words, "The hour is upon you, look not back." [6] Neither Chet nor I expected that and we both stepped quietly off the stoop without a comment. I followed him to the car, and we began our drive to Brainerd.

Our son Tony was a grown up six year old, and at first, he was a little unsure of the move. He knew that he would be leaving his favorite cousins and his grandpa and grandmas, and that we wouldn't get to see them as often. We assured him that they would be able to visit us, and we wouldn't really be that far away. We did everything to assure him that it would be fine. We talked about the beautiful lakes and Paul Bunyan and his blue ox, Babe, and some of the things we would get to do. Our youngest son was only three and just wanted to be where mom and dad and Tony were. We were all excited and looking forward to our new home, and once we were on our way, we all seemed to relax and enjoy the ride.

The move into the house was so easy. The movers were excellent and so accommodating, and the house was completely done and all cleaned and ready when we arrived. My mother came down to give us a hand, and the two of us were so organized that we were amazed at how smoothly everything went. We even had the pictures hanging on the walls by our second day.

We were the first house on our street and were eager to see the other houses finished and occupied. There were some homes on the next block, and two of the couples on that street came over to introduce themselves and welcome us to the area. We talked and shared a lot about our families and our circumstances, and seemed to hit it off right away. I was so pleased that one of the couples had two sons near the ages of ours and was anxious for them to play together and get to know one another.

After they left, Chet asked me why in the entire conversation I never mentioned Jesus. "When they asked you what you were interested in, why didn't you tell them about your prayer groups and Bible studies?" "I don't know," I said. "You know," he said, "You will have to tell them." Chet often says things that take me by surprise—this was definitely one of those times. He never seemed interested or enthused about my prayer groups or Bible studies, and we didn't talk about them with each other. What he said did impress me and I knew that I would just have to be myself with the people I met.

Chet was right about my sharing my interests with the new neighbors. Jesus was such an important part of my life that there was no way I could stay quiet. I prayed that the Lord would open me up to the new people I met and that His love would shine through me. I prayed that I would not hesitate to share with others. The very next day, He gave me an opportunity and from that point on, it seemed natural to talk about Him anywhere, and at anytime.

I answered the phone in the morning, and it was Shirley. She told me she missed me already. It was good to hear her voice and of course she had all kinds of wonderful news to share with me. Several people we knew had received healing and others had prayers answered and their needs met. By the time our conversation ended, my spirit was almost floating. I couldn't contain my happiness about all we had talked about and it just seemed to fill my whole being.

Shortly after my conversation with Shirley, I was invited to the home of one of the women I had met the night before. She called right after Shirley and asked me over for coffee. As soon as I walked into her home she commented on the fact that I was so happy looking and said that I had better tell her what was so exciting in my morning that did that for me. I took the opportunity to share some of the things that Shirley had told me plus some of the things that the Lord was doing in my life.

I knew from that moment that it would be easy to speak about Jesus anytime.

"I will counsel you and watch over you"
Psalm 32:8b

We had been in Brainerd for a month and I was already feeling the desire to become involved with a prayer group. I called one of the Catholic churches in town and found out that there was a group that met on Tuesday evenings. I had such an attachment to the wonderful friends I had made in the group I had just left—I knew I could never replace them. Their love and friendship will always hold a special place in my heart. But God's family is a great big one, and He is always introducing us to new brothers and sisters.

The welcome I experienced in the Brainerd "Living Water" prayer community was quite a surprise, and I knew that the Lord had arranged it all. As I walked into the church meeting room I looked around at the people assembled there, all talking and visiting with one another. I had no idea how to approach them and while I was thinking over a plan of action, a little nun came over to me. She smiled and said, "Hi, you must be Mary Ann Zadra. Come on in, we've been expecting you." I couldn't believe it! How could she have known me? There wasn't a single person in the group that I had ever laid eyes on before. Sister saw my surprised look and quickly explained that she had recently attended a meeting in Duluth. There, she had met several members of my old prayer group. As soon as they discovered that she was from Brainerd they began to tell her about me. They even wrote notes and cards and gave them to her. She had them all for me and had just been waiting for me to show up at one of the meetings. How quickly I relaxed, and I realized that it was just more of God's family. I felt so at home, and I had only been there a short time.

After the meeting, we had coffee and treats, and a chance to get to know one another. This neat-looking red-haired lady came over to talk to me. She said that she was very new to the group too and was anxious to get to know everyone. As we were getting acquainted, a member of the group came over to us and said, "I think I'd like to get to know the two of you better. Why don't we plan a time to get better acquainted?" Laurel invited JoAnn and I to come for coffee at her home one day during the week, and we immediately accepted her invitation.

God was so good—the way He had opened the doors for me to feel a part of the new group right away was a huge blessing, and I was looking forward to getting together with these two women. Everything seemed to be working out so well. There was only one little rough place that had me concerned, and I needed to bring it before the Lord.

I couldn't get thoughts about the house in Cherry out of my mind. It hadn't been on the market very long, but we were anxious for it to sell. We were uncomfortable leaving it empty and were concerned about vandalism; in addition, we needed the money. I prayed about it daily, but everything seemed to be at a standstill. My prayers became selfish, and instead of trusting God to handle it, I began to recite my list all of the sensible reasons that the house should sell. One night after such a prayer time I walked out of the room where I usually prayed and heard a voice say, "And, what if it should burn to the ground?" I ignored the urge to stop and pray, and just kept walking out of the room. The next morning I received a phone call from my aunt. She began to fill me in on problems my old neighbors were experiencing. It was a very dry summer, and fires had been breaking our all over the area and were becoming difficult to contain. People were hosing down their homes to keep the fire from getting to them. I told my aunt that I wasn't worried, but deep inside I felt a panicky feeling. I remembered the words from the night before and was mad at myself for not talking to God right away.

As soon as my conversation with my aunt ended, I went right to prayer. I began relisting all the reasons why we need the house to sell when suddenly I saw the situation in a different light. I prayed instead that if fire should come that it would take our empty house rather than one where people were living, or, if the house was spared, that God would give it to someone who was in need. I finished praying, leaving the situation with the Lord and believing that however He worked would be the perfect way. I felt peaceful, and the panic and turmoil left me.

That afternoon, JoAnn and I went to Laurel's for coffee. It was super! The Lord just breaks down all kinds of barriers, and with Him as our common denominator, we felt as if we had known one another for years. Laurel was a terrific hostess and her home was so comfortable—a perfect atmosphere for relaxing. We enjoyed it so much that when we finally focused on the time we were amazed how quickly it had flown by. We knew that this was the beginning of a friendship that would still be intact in eternity. Before we left Laurel's, we prayed, and something happened during that prayer time that I wasn't expecting at all.

I had made it a practice to listen to others and to focus in on the prayers they were saying so I could pray along with them. This time, however, it was as if I had no choice. I could hear Laurel praying, but I couldn't concentrate on what she was saying. I had my eyes closed and a picture appeared in my mind like on huge television screen. I saw the house in Cherry as clearly as if I were in the front yard. I could see fire coming up the grass and moving up the tree trunks. It was blazing and I could almost feel the heat, but it did not touch the house. It only came up to it and surrounded it, then it continued to move on past, lifting up into the sky. Next, I became aware that a car had come into the driveway. I didn't see it, but I knew it was there. I saw four people walking up the sidewalk: a man and a woman and two children. They had suitcases and were carrying them into the house. Then suddenly the pictures were gone and I could hear Laurel and JoAnn praying. I didn't share what had just happened to me. I was embarrassed that my thoughts were so far away from the prayers they were saying.

I came home to a ringing telephone and went to pick it up as soon as I had closed the door. It was the Realtor who was dealing with our house in Cherry. He informed me that the house had just been sold to a couple with two children. He shared a few details and points that needed to be discussed; he would be calling soon to take care of them.

As soon as our conversation ended, I began to praise and thank God for all He had done. I was so glad that God had given me the opportunity to get things right with Him and to release the house to Him and to leave it there, trusting Him for whatever happened.

> "I will lead the blind by ways they have not known, along unfamiliar paths I will guide them; I will turn the darkness into light before them and make the rough places smooth."
> Isaiah 42:16

Getting Involved

I was enjoying meeting neighbors and attending the new prayer group, but I had a desire to do a Bible study on my own. I thought I would begin in Matthew and move through the New Testament, but the Lord impressed upon me that I should begin in Mark. I, of course, thought my way was better—after all, it made more sense to begin at the beginning. The Lord still seemed insistent that I begin in Mark. As I was mulling over this decision, the telephone rang. It was a woman that I had recently been introduced to at prayer group. "We're starting up a Bible study and we'd like you to come." I told her that I was about to begin a study on my own, but as soon as she said, "Oh, please, it will be really good, we're starting in the gospel of Mark," I responded with an "I'll be there!" I had a feeling that the Lord had a big grin on His face. I knew that my little episode earlier was leading me into accepting this invitation to participate in the Bible study.

The study turned out to be one of a series of Stonecroft Bible Studies and Laurel was leading it. Her sweet spirit and love of Jesus was so evident and her teaching and leadership so good that I was glad I had become involved, and I knew I was right where I was supposed to be. As I began to get to know the others who had committed to the study, I was blessed by their enthusiasm for God's Word and their love of Jesus. Throughout the weeks of that first study, Laurel asked all of us to consider becoming a study leader. I thought that several of the women who attended would be great at it, so I prayed for them. God, however, had a different plan, and soon I found myself involved with leading studies in the Stonecroft Bible Groups.

I was becoming more involved in my regular prayer group too. It was so easy, and everyone was so nice to be with, you couldn't help but want to do more—and there was a great deal to do. Greeting new people, serving the coffee, setting up and tearing down tables and chairs, prayer needs, music, etc. Each ministry was vital to the smooth operation of the meeting. I became involved with the telephone prayer ministry, but right from the start, I felt that God had something else for me to do. I had only been involved with the phone ministry for a short while when the Lord began to speak to me about a different work.

The Lord had spoken to me about a teaching ministry when I was attending prayer groups prior to moving to Brainerd, but nothing had ever materialized. Now, the Lord began to speak to me in the same way. "There is a life ahead which you could not have entered before. There is a work ready for you; I have prepared you for it." I was a bit doubtful. I wasn't into the Word as much as I should have been and I hadn't been in the group a whole year yet. It didn't seem as though being in the teaching ministry at this time would be possible.

One day during prayer, the Lord impressed upon me that a man named Al who held a leadership position in the group would be asking me to give a teaching. I was to tell him that I would. Not a thing happened at the meeting that night, and I began to think that I had misunderstood, or that I had this idea in my head and God had not really spoken to me at all. Throughout the following week, the Lord kept giving me the same message. Needless to say, I was a bit confused. The following meeting arrived and I was anxious to attend as usual. This time, Al came up to me immediately. He said he had tried several times the previous week to speak to me, but there were so many interruptions and when he finally had time, I had already left. He told me that the Lord had been urging him to ask me to give a teaching. Al said that he had prayed with the other coordinators and they all agreed. I was excited and I told Al that I would be happy to participate in the teaching ministry. I was totally unprepared when he then said that I would be giving the next teaching and that I was to give it on anything the Lord led me to.

> **"He will keep in perfect peace
> all those who trust in Him,
> whose thoughts turn often to the Lord."**
> **Isaiah 26:3**

The very next morning it dawned on me that I had absolutely nothing to say, and I began to get cold feet. What possible teaching could I give to the group, and how in the world could I fill twenty or thirty minutes? By late afternoon I had worked myself into quite a state. I was preparing supper and talking to the Lord.

"Lord, this is Your work. You got me into this; in fact, I am not at all prepared and cannot do a thing unless You help me. You're going to have to tell me what to talk about. I want to be open to You and yielded to whatever You say."

On one of my shopping trips to a Christian book store I had purchased a little plastic bread loaf with an opening on top that contained about 100 Scripture cards. I had never used them, and they sat on the corner of the stove like a decoration. As I was praying and talking to Jesus, I looked at that little loaf and reached to pull out a card. It said, "Teach My people the difference between the holy and the profane, and cause them to discern between wrong and right." (Ezekiel 44:23) "Oh, Jesus, how am I going to do that?" I took out another card and read, "Fear thou not, for I am with thee. Be not dismayed for I am thy God, I will strengthen thee, yeah, I will help thee." (Isaiah 41:10) I later was reading my daily devotional and was very encouraged to read the words, "Be My mouth piece and I will supply the words and the message."

During the week the Lord revealed many Scriptures on holiness, and the teaching began to take shape. It was no effort on my part; even the typing was a breeze. It was as though I just sat watching the Lord do the work. When I finished it, I read it over. I took a break before getting into my regular chores and decided to read a little from *Come Away My Beloved.* The words I read were, "Lo, I say unto thee, be not intimidated by anyone, but speak forth My Word even as I have given it unto thee. Ye have written freely and fearlessly, now speak in the same way. I will be with thee and keep thy mouth, trust Me." [7]

Praise God! He is so wonderful! He really means it when He says He will do it all. All things are in His hands, and I was realizing it more and more each day. That night as I gave the teaching, I experienced the Lord at work. I opened with a prayer and as soon as it was done, I almost felt as if I was standing next to myself observing the teaching. The Holy Spirit really took over and did it all!

And, He did it for every teaching I ever did.

> **"We know how much God loves us,
> because we have felt His love"**
> I John 4:16

The Lord blessed me in many ways. Allowing me to be a part of the prayer group and permitting me to share through the teaching ministry was incredible, and I was constantly learning more things. I was so comfortable with my brothers and sisters in Christ and happy to be a part of God's family. In addition to my working with others, the Lord was also letting them minister to me through their love, sharing, encouragement and thoughtfulness. My friendship with JoAnn had grown into something very special, and her influence in my life was profound. I knew she turned to the Lord for wisdom and guidance and He often used her to shed light on a particular situation. I could always count on her perspective and advice.

I struggled with a negative attitude toward myself. I continually belittled myself in front of others. This behavior had become a bad habit and I didn't realize the degree to which I was doing it. It was hard for me to accept a compliment. If someone said that I looked nice I never just said "thank you," but would make a negative comment on the fact that I needed a haircut, or my outfit was ancient. My family did the same thing, so I was used to that kind of response and behavior. I was always apologizing to everyone. When I had company, I apologized for the dust or the way the house looked, even if I had just cleaned. If I was serving a meal, I apologized for each thing I served—the roast was too done, too stringy, or too tough; the salad had too much vinegar, or not enough. The dessert was too firm or not firm enough—and on and on! When I went visiting I would make a negative comment that immediately called attention to myself: "I hope you don't mind how I look, I just threw this old thing on," and so on. I think besides being a habit, there was a part of me that feared rejection or criticism from others—if I said it first, it was okay.

Pride is a trap we often fall into without even realizing it. It is foolish to think that we are the center of attention. If I walked into a room with ten other people in it, I would think that they were evaluating me as soon as they saw me. In truth, they were probably more focused on themselves. I once heard about a man who went to a football game—when the team got into a huddle, the man thought they were talking about him. I know what that feels like. I did not have a good view of truth when it concerned me, but the Lord was working in this area of my life, and slowly but surely changes were taking place.

We all need to feel good about ourselves and develop a healthy attitude and wholesome outlook, not one that is self-centered and full of pride. Through the light of the Word, I began to understand this, and I also began to learn that I was a person that mattered. The first chapter of Ephesians shows us what our position is in Christ and how very important we are in God's plan. God sees us in a way that we do not see ourselves. He chose us before the foundations of the world, adopted us into His family, showered us with the Holy Spirit. We belong to Him.

The Lord began to open my eyes to see the way I viewed myself and how I needed to change to an attitude that reflected His truth. I couldn't protect myself from the criticism of others by criticizing myself and focusing on me—to do that is self-centered, and self-love. One day, a person I did not even know overheard me and approached me. He asked me why I had such a negative attitude about myself. Following this experience, I encountered several friends and neighbors that made the same observation. Since it all occurred in a very small time frame, I began to think about it. I asked Chet if he had noticed it and he confirmed that on many occasions I did display a very negative and critical attitude about myself. Just the way it all came to a head and from so many different people, I sense that the Lord was behind it. I began to pray earnestly that my attitude toward myself would change.

The first thing that happened after that prayer occurred on a drive I took with JoAnn. I was telling her how the Lord had been dealing with me and how He had used others to reveal my attitude to me and my self-focus. Suddenly, JoAnn looked at me and began to tell me how she felt about me and what she thought of me. In that moment, a veil was lifted from my eyes and God allowed me to see the genuine love in JoAnn. It overwhelmed me that she liked me just for myself. She loved me with

Jesus' love. I couldn't help but cry. I could not have imagined her liking me just because I'm me.

After that day, the lack of self-worth, critical attitude, and self-focus seemed to leave. I became more confident and had a more positive and healthy view of myself. I began to feel special—not in a way that generates pride, but in the way God intended. He replaced my negative view with a love for myself that I never had experienced before. Along with the changes in how I felt towards myself came a joy in loving others that was a freer, more honest love—not based on any comparisons, flaws, attitudes or misconceptions on my part, but rather with the love and acceptance that God instilled in me. I loved them just because I loved them.

Following the lessons I had learned, the changes that occurred in me, and the new love that I found for others came the reality that God wanted me to see everyone under the shed blood of Christ. He wanted me to clearly understand that He died for everyone. It is so easy to see Him in other believers, but with those who do not know Him, we often have a different response. On a number of occasions I caught myself referring to those who weren't born again as "the heathen" forgetting that Jesus paid the same price for them as He did for me. How differently I look at it now because of Him. I began to look for something good and positive in everyone I met. God accepts us just as we are. He showed me how to accept myself, and then He began to show me how special others were. God commands us to love one another. He doesn't say we should love only those dear to our hearts or those who share a common bond with us, He says we should love *everyone.* That's a pretty tall order, and it is totally impossible without Jesus.

> "Dear friends, let us love one another, for love comes from God. Everyone who loves has been born of God and knows God. Whoever does not love does not know God, for God is love." I John 4:7-8

Let Your Light Shine

Jesus was changing my heart and teaching me how to really love others. At the same time, He was increasing my desire to witness. He had done so much for me, and I wanted to share His love with others that they too might experience His salvation. I shared my desire with Him and He began to bring people into my life that I could talk to.

I had been praying for a neighbor of mine for some time, and finally, I had the opportunity to tell her about Jesus. She was very receptive to the things I shared and when the chance came I invited her to attend a Full Gospel meeting. She agreed to come with me. That night, after the meeting, she invited Christ into her life to be her Lord and Savior.

We always included music in our prayer meetings and one evening we sang the words "This little light of mine, I'm going to let it shine, let it shine let it shine, let it shine. Shine all over my neighborhood, I'm going to let it shine." For some reason, the lyrics kept playing themselves in my mind and as soon as I got in the car to drive home, I began singing. The area we lived in was very dark. We did not have a single streetlight, and when there were no lights on in the houses, it was pitch black. As I was singing, I turned the corner onto our street and suddenly, a bright light lit up the whole neighborhood.

Chet and I had acquired an old street lamp and had intended to put it up in our front yard. We never got around to wiring it—too many other projects, I guess. Chet had gotten home early and decided to surprise me, and what a surprise it was! Just as I turned the corner singing, "Let it shine all over my neighborhood" the light came on and I could see how just one light could make a huge difference. It dispelled the darkness in a moment. I thought this coincidence was wonderful and when I sat down to say my evening prayers, I mentioned it to the Lord. There was a devotional on the desk and I opened it up to read the day's message. You guessed it: "You are the world's light, a city on a hill, glowing in the night for all to see. Don't hide your light! Let it shine for all." (Matthew 5:14-15)

God showed me that even if you are the only Christian (the only "light") in your family, neighborhood, workplace, or club, He has you there for a reason. We need to pray about the people we are in contact with and be open to share as God leads. The light of Christ in us will have an effect on them, even if we are never given the opportunity to speak to them about the Lord. If we do have a chance to witness, we do not have to be afraid. God is the one who draws people to Him, and the Holy Spirit speaks to their hearts.

"How lovely on the mountains are the feet of those who bring good news"
Isaiah 52:7

There was an elderly gentleman who attended prayer group, a retired Baptist minister who really knew the Word of God. Whenever he talked about Jesus, his face would just glow. One evening, he gave the teaching. His appearance was always so neat—white hair perfectly combed, dressed in a tailored suit, white shirt and tie. In addition to his impeccable appearance, his teachings were inspiring and moving. This particular evening, I couldn't help but think how beautifully he spoke, how well he taught the Scriptures and life lessons he had learned through the years. That, coupled with his appearance, was striking indeed. I was engrossed in his teaching when suddenly my eyes drifted to his feet and I almost gasped out loud. He was wearing brand new tennis shoes! They were gleaming white and had the thickest rubber soles I ever saw. It was in such contrast to the rest of his clothing that I couldn't help but wonder whatever possessed him to choose them as an accessory to his otherwise perfect ensemble.

I didn't realize it, but before the teaching started, I had opened my Bible. I glanced down at it and could hardly contain myself as I read, "How beautiful upon the mountains are the feet of those who bring the happy news of peace and salvation, the news that the God of Israel reigns." (Isaiah 52:7) It was the Lord's way of showing me that we don't have to be ordained ministers or teachers, or Bible scholars. It matters not if we are in expensive shoes, sandals, or tennis shoes. God can use us to spread His Word. Our feet can be those spoken of in Isaiah—we can be God's messengers!

"Refrain from anger..."
Psalm 37:8

Before we can truly be effective in our Christian witness, before we can "shine out," we have to be certain that our lives are in order. So often things occur in our lives that dull our Christian witness and cloud our lights. Many times we build barriers between us and others, leading to a barrier between us and God. These walls must be torn down before we can be fruitful. We need to repent of our wrongdoing and confess our sin to the Lord.

The Lord revealed an attitude of mine that needed to be taken care of before I could move on. It was an attitude that I was unaware of, but God revealed it to me one afternoon.

Chet and I were entertaining guests, and in the middle of our visiting I received a phone call from an aunt of mine. I was so glad to hear her voice, but my reaction to what she said surprised us both. She told me that a party was being planned for my grandma's birthday and wanted to know if I would help. Her request was simple enough, but I just flipped. A flood of memories came surging into my mind and I replied sharply, "I don't want a thing to do with it! I prefer to come as a guest and not be involved with anything else. If I can send money for my share, fine; otherwise, leave me out of any of the planning!" I could feel anger rising within me and tears burning hot in my eyes. No way would I ever take part in this, not after what had happened to me before. My aunt had no idea at all what was motivating me to act this way. I could tell by her voice that she was hurt by my response. I was so involved with my own feelings that I didn't even think of hers. I hung up the phone. I was just shaking and my heart was pounding a mile a minute.

I hadn't thought about my grandma's 88th birthday for a long time, but the phone call reminded me of what had taken place then. My grandma was one of those very special people, and when she was 88 years old everyone decided to surprise her with a party. The family got together to do the planning, and since I had a lot of free time, I volunteered to do the invitations, set up the date, arrange for the restaurant, and select the menu. Everyone pitched in to pay for the party.

We invited 60 people, and since the restaurant was doing all of the setting up and catering, we knew that we would have a perfect time celebrating with grandma and visiting with the guests.

The party started off beautifully, and I know that for just about everyone there, it stayed that way. For me, however, it turned into a nightmare. Shortly after the party had gotten underway, I was notified by a guest that there was a problem in the kitchen. I went in and found one of the waitresses in tears. The manager of the restaurant was standing there silently as he looked at a lady going through his cooler. She moved cans and bottles around while she screamed about the poor planning. It seemed that a certain kind of beverage had not been provided for the party. She swore at everyone in earshot. I couldn't believe the whole scene. The manager reluctantly apologized to the woman and she finally quieted down. I was embarrassed that one of our invited guests had been so rude and abusive. I told the manager that I was sorry for the incident and I expressed my regrets to the waitress. She was still quite shaken, but mumbled that it was okay.

As soon as I walked out of the kitchen, someone grabbed my arm and said that their table was running out of appetizers and would I please take care of it. Before I could respond, a relative came up to me and chided me that we had booked a restaurant that closed the bar at 4:00. She announced loudly that she had paid her share for the party and I had just better get a move on and fix it so it would stay open. I tried to explain that the arrangements for serving refreshments and food had been set by the management of the restaurant and that we had all agreed on it ahead of time.

My head was just spinning by this time. I tried to take a breath and collect my thoughts when an aunt of mine came over to me and ordered me to get a move on and see that the food was put out immediately. I told her that the kitchen had already been instructed to begin serving at 4:30. She said that I should just ignore that and march right in there and tell them to speed it up. I was telling her that I couldn't do that when one of her children came up to me and said to just shut up and do what her mother wanted me to do.

I couldn't take another minute of all that I was exposed to in that short span of time, and I just had to get out of there. As I passed a table on my way to the restroom, someone grabbed my arm and said, "Oh, miss, would you fix us up with a round." It was all I could do to just keep walking. I didn't want to spoil the party by crying, but I could tell that is exactly what I was very close to doing.

One of the guests had seen everything that had taken place and she ran after me. She gave me a hug and it really encouraged me to receive her support. She talked with me and calmed me down; she even prayed with me. I began to understand that each person felt that their requests were legitimate and none of them had been aware of what else was going on. When it all hit me at once, I felt like a trapped rabbit and all I wanted to do was escape.

After I calmed down, I came out of the restroom. My stomach was still uncomfortable and I didn't dare eat anything. I was even reluctant to talk because I was afraid I might say something inappropriate. I was surprised when several of the guests came over to me during the rest of the party. They had observed what had happened and were sorry that I had to endure the mistreatment from so many at once.

The people who were visiting us when my aunt called happened to be guests at the party and had been witness to everything that had been taken place. After my aunt's call, I came before them, explained what she had called about, and then relived the entire incident before them, and boy, was I angry. I had a right to be upset after all, and after the way I'd been hurt and mistreated, they should have been the ones who apologized to me! I went on and on. Suddenly, I realized what I was saying and how I had been acting. What was wrong with me—what kind of person was I anyway? Where was the forgiveness in my heart?

Over the next few days, Jesus began to reveal Scriptures on forgiveness to me. He also showed me the need for repentance in my own life. I had taken everything that had happened that night as a personal attack. I never once considered another person's feelings. The woman shouting in the kitchen may have had good reason, and each person in turn may have been right in their request. I had only observed things from my limited understanding of where each was coming from. I realized how I had allowed Satan to take advantage of the situation.

Instead of a quiet spirit and Christ-like light, I displayed a spirit of anger and bitterness. When I finally recognized my own sin, I prayed, "Give me a broken spirit and a contrite heart; open my eyes that I can see the beam in them and realize my own sin; teach me, Lord, to live in love and to learn to forgive from my heart."

I was truly sorry for the way I had kept unforgiveness in my heart towards so many people for such a long time. They had no idea they had done anything to me, yet, I had carried resentment and bitter feelings within my heart. One by one, as the Lord brought them to my mind, I imagined standing face to face with them. I asked each one to forgive me and I forgave them. I asked God's forgiveness too, and I asked Him to heal my heart and my attitude.

"And when you stand praying, forgive, if you have ought to against any; that your Father also which is in Heaven may forgive you your trespasses. But, if you do not forgive, neither will your Father which is in Heaven forgive your trespasses." (Mark 11:25-26) The Bible also tells us in Psalm 34:18 that "The Lord is close to those whose hearts are breaking and are humbly sorry for their sins."

I was thankful for the way the Lord worked. Since these things had occurred within me, and since it had happened so long ago, He permitted the repentance and forgiveness to take place in my prayer time with Him. Repentance—confession—forgiveness. When we see how quick to forgive us that the Lord is, we in turn should show that same attitude toward others. The only one I had to apologize to was my aunt who had made the phone call. When I saw her and asked her to forgive me for the way I acted, she did. I'm sure she didn't understand all that had taken place, but I knew after speaking to her that all was just fine between us.

We can become self-righteous so quickly. Pride can bring us into judgment of others, closing us off to God's voice speaking to us. I minimized my own part in everything by blaming everyone else. When we don't recognize our sin and repent of it, we block our relationship with God and with the people in our lives. Our Christian witness becomes dull and our light is hidden. Often, the things we do seem small and hardly worth recognizing, but if they have a chance to grow and build up, we can slip away from a closeness to our Heavenly Father. In

Matthew 18:21-22, Peter asks Jesus, "How often shall my brother sin against me, and I forgive him? Seven times?" Jesus said to Peter, "I say not unto thee until seven times, but until seventy times seven."

Many times I have reflected on the reason I went through this experience. The Lord revealed several things to me. One is that we all have a need to be understood and treated fairly. I believe we go through times like this so we can sympathize, comfort, and understand others who are dealing with similar situations. I also learned lessons concerning anger. When injustice is done, we should speak out against it. Whenever there is something morally wrong, unjust, or violent, we cannot stand silent; but when our anger is directed toward individuals in a selfish and misguided manner, then it is wrong. In my case, I may have been mistreated, but my reaction was one of criticism, bitterness, and self-pity, all against people who did not even know they had done anything. Anger can destroy us when it is hateful and is allowed to fester. Without my own experience with anger and hurt, I could not have understood the beautiful lessons in forgiveness and the healing that comes through our confession and repentance, the peace that comes from God's pardon, and the joy that occurs in a restored relationship. We have to take positive steps not only to receive it, but to be able to forgive. "If we confess our sins, He is faithful and just to forgive us our sins and to cleanse us from all unrighteousness." (I John 1:9) In addition to forgiving us, the Bible tells us that He forgets our transgressions, and we are to do the same. We cannot just say we have forgiven someone and then continue to dwell on it. We must sincerely mean it—we must forgive, and forget.

> **"And I am sure that God who began the good work within you
> will keep right on helping you to grow in His grace
> until His task within you is finally finished
> on that day when Jesus Christ returns."
> Philippians 1:6**

We had been in Brainerd for several months, and I was getting more involved with the Catholic church. I still entertained the idea of leaving, and I felt that the Lord would show me when the time was right. I was involved with the prayer community and even though it was basically Catholic, there were also people from the Lutheran, Episcopalian, and Assemblies of God churches.

One afternoon I came home from shopping to find a strange car in my yard. An elderly couple had been sitting in the car. As soon as I got out of my car, they stepped out of theirs. They told me they had felt led to come to my house. It had been quite a hectic day for them and they were beginning to get a little tired. They had been going around to homes in our area to tell them about a chapel that they were opening in our vicinity. The chapel had not been in use for some time, but this man and his wife felt led by the Lord to do something about it. He was a retired Baptist minister and had felt a strong desire to preach and teach in the chapel. We talked for a long time and prayed together. After they left, I thought that maybe this was the door the Lord was opening for me and I decided to pray daily for the couple, their vision for the chapel, and for God's guidance for me. In the meantime, I would continue to attend mass at the Catholic church, and get to services at the Assemblies of God as often as I could.

Shortly after the elderly couple had visited with me, I received an invitation from them. They were now holding services at the chapel and wanted me to come to hear a speaker who was a representative for a Bible-translating fellowship. I accepted the invitation, and was very glad that I did. It was good to see the couple again, and I was blessed by the joy and happiness displayed by the people there. The talk the speaker gave was very interesting and the slides he brought gave great insight into what his ministry was doing. Only one thing in his presentation bothered me. He showed slides of a group of natives he had the privilege of working with on one of his missionary trips. He explained that in the past, Catholic missionaries had come to these people and taught them the Catholic beliefs, about holy days, and the various saints and rituals. The gospel was never preached, and souls were not won for the Lord. What did happen was that the natives kept the holy days but adapted them to their own style, paganized them and used them to worship their own idols. I knew that God had a reason for me to see the presentation, and that there would come a time when I would no longer be able to be a part of the Catholic church. I also knew that for the present, I was not to leave. I believed that God wanted me to stay for the very purpose of sharing the gospel with any who were open.

I had an opportunity following this experience to visit with a Catholic priest. He was a born-again, spirit-filled Christian. We prayed together and talked for a long time. He understood what I was feeling and was able to be encouraging and helpful to me. He told me that I needed to be patient, to stay in an attitude of prayer, and to be open to the Lord's leading. He agreed that there was a purpose to my remaining in the church and that when the time was right, Jesus would let me know. He also told me that when the time came, I would have perfect peace about it.

Even though I was to remain in the church, I believed that the Lord wanted my main association to be with the prayer group. During prayer, He stressed the importance of unity, of standing together, praying for one another, and encouraging one another. I needed to be with those who were like-minded, and I needed to be open to the Lord so He could use me where He had placed me. I was a member of the core group and we were responsible for coordinating the meetings. We took turns giving teachings and leading prayer in small-group situations. There were always special needs to pray for and we would meet in a smaller room to pray after each meeting. This was my favorite place to be—Jesus blessed us so much during this time. Prayers were answered, healing took place, people accepted Jesus as Lord and Savior—it was so powerful!

I remember one night in particular. Five of us were praying for a woman with a serious physical need. We barely laid hands on her and began to pray when she began shaking. It was almost as if currents of electricity were flowing through us to her. I felt the presence of the Lord so strongly that I could hardly remain on my feet. A couple of others who were praying were slain in the spirit, but each time I felt myself falling, I braced myself against it. God's power was very evident and the woman was healed.

Following the meeting, I was angry with myself for refusing God's blessing. I knew that I, too, would have been slain in the spirit if I had not fought the feeling. I promised the Lord that I would never again say "no" to the Holy Spirit when He moved in this way, but that I would remain open to whatever He had in store.

Several weeks later, I was entertaining a guest, and she and I decided to go to the Assemblies of God to hear a man named Richard Shakarian speak. I had never heard him, but I had read a book by his father, Demos Shakarian, called *The Happiest People on Earth.* It is so wonderful to get together with other believers to praise and worship the Lord, and that night was no exception. The talk by Richard was inspiring, and you could sense his love for the Lord. There were 300 people present, all worshipping the Lord in prayer and song. It was truly uplifting, and during the worship, one person was slain in the spirit. I couldn't believe it. Unlike the night at the prayer meeting, I had no chance to refuse. Jesus swept me right off of my feet. His presence was so strong that there was no way I could have remained standing. Waves and waves of His love passed over me. The feeling was incredible and I could have remained like that forever. I did not find out until later that I had been the only one to experience the Lord in this way at that meeting. I knew that He had done it deliberately, and I also knew that whatever He chose to do with me from then on was okay with me.

> **"Therefore, if anyone is in Christ,
> he is a new creation;
> the old has gone, the new has come!"
> 2 Corinthians 5:17**

Tony, our eldest son, was preparing to go through first communion instructions with his CCD class. The church program was set up around the family, and parental involvement was extremely important. The parents would be responsible to teach and direct their own children to get them ready for communion. (This was new to me—when I was growing up, we relied on the priest and the nuns to instruct us.) Classes for the parents were set to meet several times over a two-month period to receive information from the parish priest, discuss the evening's topic and compare notes. We were also to gather materials to pass on to our children. Chet and I attended the first two sessions, missed the next session, then I came alone to the fourth session because Chet was working late.

When we were at the first two sessions, everyone was able to share their opinion on the issues that were discussed. I shared whenever I felt the Holy Spirit prompting me to do so. I arrived a few minutes late the evening of the fourth session. Everyone had already divided into small groups of 6 - 8 parents and I sat down with one of the groups. The priest who normally led the introductory teaching was unable to be there, but left instructions for us to review the previous week's lesson and discuss any material that had been presented since the sessions had started. Evidently, the Priest had chosen to speak on the Old Testament, and that was what the group had been discussing.

I listened with amazement as they explained that he had told them that most of the Old Testament was made up of stories that were not true, but were told for the purpose of instruction. The walls tumbling down, Noah's Ark, the burning bush, the parting of the water, Jonah and the whale—they were simply stories told for the sake of a lesson or to illustrate a point. He had an explanation for each story—for example, when the Nile River became red with blood (Exodus 7:20-21) it was really ore in the water that made it look that way. The group was discussing the lesson casually and they agreed that telling stories was a good way to teach a lesson. I almost jumped out of my seat!

Shortly before I left for the meeting the Lord told me to take a Bible with me. No one had brought a Bible to any of the other meetings and I was curious as to why I was to bring one now. In addition, I was impressed to bring a brand new Bible that I had recently purchased rather than take my regular one. Now, as I listened to the comments around me, I was glad that I had it with me. I told them that I held a different opinion than the one offered by the priest. I said that I believed that the Bible was the Word of God and the writings were not simple stories, but the truth. I was asked several questions and each time God gave me Scripture verses to back up what I told them. I did not say a whole lot, but I gave them as many Scriptures as the Lord gave me. Colossians 2:8 says "Don't let others spoil your faith and joy with their philosophies and their wrong and shallow answers built on man's thoughts and ideas instead of what Christ has said." II Timothy 3:6 tells us that "The whole Bible is given to us by inspiration of God and is profitable for doctrine, for reproof, for correction, and for instruction in righteousness." I told the group that I would keep them in my prayers and I urged each one there to not take the priest's word as the final one, but to look to God—they would find the right answers by turning to Jesus and allowing Him to teach them.

The meeting ended and I was on the way to my car when one of the parents came up to me. We chatted a bit about the session and he told me that he noticed a difference between me and the others that were there. He said that he had listened to some of the things I shared at the first few sessions and he had been thinking about what I had said. He asked me to tell him what it was that made me different and how he could have that too. I followed the Lord's leading and invited him into the car with me for a few minutes. I told him that we are separated from God by our sins and that we all need to receive His forgiveness. I told him that God sent His only Son into the world to atone for our sins on the cross, that Jesus is the way and the truth and the life, and that salvation is through Him alone. We cannot earn our way to Heaven and we cannot please God or come to Him in any other manner. I asked him if he had ever made a commitment to Jesus, if he had ever invited Him into his life. He said that he hadn't, but that he wanted to. We prayed a commitment prayer and I gave him the Bible that Jesus told me to bring with me.

I love how the Lord works, don't you? It is so incredible how everything falls into place and works out perfectly. I haven't seen this man or spoken to him since, but I know that Jesus worked in him that night and will continue to work in his life. "And I am sure that God who began the good work within you will keep right on helping you to grow in His grace until His task within you is finally finished on that day when Jesus Christ returns." (Philippians 1:6)

God doesn't always use us in the same way. We might be given the opportunity to plant the seed in someone's mind, but another person may come along and do the watering, and finally someone else may be used by God to do the reaping. However the Lord chooses to use us, we can be sure of one thing—when the time is right, the Holy Spirit will move in a person's heart, and they, too, will become part of the family of God.

> "Look around you! Vast fields of human souls are ripening all around and are ready for reaping. The reapers will be paid good wages and will be gathering eternal souls into the graineries of Heaven. What joys await the sower and the reaper both together. For it is true that one sows, and someone else reaps. I sent you to reap where you didn't sow; others did the work, and you received the harvest." John 4:35-38

God Will Make a Way

God showed me through a number of circumstances that He is concerned about absolutely everything in our lives. God used two separate experiences to bring this truth home to me. He can arrange the events in our lives to provide for a particular need.

Brainerd was about 147 miles away from where we had lived before and we made it a point to visit our families as often as possible. On one of our visits, I stopped in at a Christian bookstore and purchased a set of 16 New Testament tapes. When we returned home we were plunged into several very busy weeks. I had difficulty finding time to listen to the tapes. When I finally did get the opportunity to listen to the first few, I was very disappointed. They each had defects of one sort or another—they skipped portions of sentences, garbled speech, etc.

Chet and I were scheduled to make another trip to visit our families and I wanted to listen to all of the tapes so I could return the faulty ones to the bookstore. The Friday we were to leave rolled around so quickly that I knew I would never get to listen to the tapes I had left. I turned the situation over to the Lord and left it with Him. When Chet came home from work that day he had a small package with him. "You'll never guess what I bought today! I had to stop at the store and I saw one of those attachments for listening to a tape recorder in the car. I might never even use it, but for some reason, I just had to buy it today." *Praise the Lord,* I thought. *That is exactly what I need so I can listen to the tapes in the car.*

There was still one hurdle to overcome: Chet and the kids were never interested in my Christian tapes or any Christian radio I listened to. I knew if I mentioned using the attachment to listen to my tapes there would be a good amount of grumbling and complaining. I also knew that if God had provided the means, He had a plan to take care of the details. I told Chet about the tapes and asked if he would mind my listening to them on the trip. He told me to go ahead, he wouldn't mind at all. Even the kids didn't whine a bit when I turned them on as we drove out of the driveway. The tapes played the entire two and a half hours from our house to my mother's front door, and just as we stopped the car, the tapes were finished.

Another situation occurred shortly after my "tape episode." Chet had been meeting with a group of people from one of the counties he sold machinery to. The situation seemed to be an impossible one. He knew that his bid was too high and there were several people on the board who were not moved to accept his company's proposal. He worked hard on his initial presentation, but met with considerable opposition. I knew that he was worried and turning the situation around seemed impossible.

A friend and I were in the habit of meeting for prayer, and I asked her to meet with me in prayer for Chet. We asked the Lord for a miracle and prayed that he would be able to go to the meeting and not have to say a word. We prayed that everything would go smoothly and that it would be resolved in his favor. The night the meeting was scheduled, Chet had to force himself to go. He had already faced so much opposition that he saw absolutely no chance that he would even be allowed to speak again and review his presentation. He went to the meeting only out of a sense of duty.

When he returned from the meeting, he was grinning from ear to ear. His bid had been accepted and he did not have the utter a single word. A man who Chet was acquainted with (and who wasn't even involved in the proceedings) came to the meeting and spoke on Chet's behalf. Those who had previously opposed the proposal and the high bid changed their minds, and the entire board voted unanimously to accept Chet's bid. Chet just sat there and witnessed the whole thing. He was still shaking his head in amazement a week later.

It is so wonderful and reassuring to know that Jesus cares for everything concerning us. How big or how small a problem is, or how urgent or how unimportant, is not a factor for Jesus. He is with us always, in every way. We can "cast all of our anxiety on Him, because He cares for us." (I Peter 5:7)

> **"Now faith is being sure of what we hope for,
> and certain of what we do not see."
> Hebrews 11:1**

I have already shared that I had ceased dropping gospel tracts on the floor for Chet to trip over, pick up, and read. I turned him over to the Lord and knew that He would be working in Chet's life in many ways. I also knew that He would use many different experiences to witness to and minister to Chet. I continued to be faithful in my daily prayers for Chet, and during my times of prayer for him, I would often be led to Scriptures like II Peter 1:9 which reads: "God delivered him from the old life of sin so that now he can live a strong good life for the Lord." Occasionally, the Lord would bless me through readings like this one in *Come Away My Beloved.* [8]

> "Oh, My child, I have loved thee with an everlasting love, and with strong cords have I bound thee to Me. In the day of adversity, I have been thy refuge, and in the hour of need I have holden thee up, and thou has found thy strength in Me. Thou has seen my goodness on the right hand and on the left. Thou has beheld My power and My glory has not been hid from thee. I have blessed thee out of the bounties of Heaven and have not withheld from thee ought of what thy heart hath desired. Yea, and I would yet do more. For have I not promised that thou shouldest be saved AND thy household? And was not the blood applied to the lintel and the door posts to the salvation of the entire family? (Exodus 12:22-23)

> "So renew thy energies, and know that I am working with thee. For surely a light shall shine out of the darkness and the faith thou hast exercised through the years shall be rewarded an hundred-fold. So thy faith shall be turned to sight; for thou shalt see with thine eyes and hear with thine ears and rejoice in thine heart over that thing which shall come to pass. I will do a wonderful work, and thou shalt praise and glorify my name TOGETHER!

"For He that keepeth thee neither slumbers nor sleeps. The Lord thy God is thy strength and in Him is no weariness. He tireth not at thy coming and thy cry is welcome to His ears however frequent. Cast thyself upon His mercies; for His loving-kindness never faileth, and His grace and compassion are inexhaustible. His faithfulness is extended to all generations."
Isaiah 59:21

There is no doubt in my mind that God is using all of these messages to reassure me that He is at work and there will come a day when I will see my husband come into a relationship with Him. "What is faith? It is the confident assurance that something we want is going to happen. It is the certainty that what we hope for is waiting for us, even though we cannot see it up ahead." (Hebrews 11:1)

I had received these messages and others just before Chet was about to celebrate a birthday. Early in the day, we had a little celebration with the boys, but in the evening, Chet and I went out to eat together. Going out to eat was not an uncommon event—we often went out with the boys or with friends, or with our family when they visited. What made it different was that we went alone, and surprise of surprises, our conversation even turned to spiritual things. The evening was perfect and I went to bed imagining that there was more to come.

I expected Chet to wake up in the morning shouting "Praise the Lord," but of course, that did not happen. What did happen was not at all what I had envisioned. It was Sunday and I had to spend the afternoon at the laundromat because our drain at home had been plugged. I got the machines started and then sat in a chair by the window. I was alone in the place, so I began talking to the Lord. I told Him that I had really expected something to happen in Chet's spiritual life. Everything I had been reading, our conversation on spiritual things, and the way his birthday evening had turned out didn't seem to have affected Chet at all spiritually.

At that point in my conversation with the Lord, I spotted a magazine on the windowsill across the room. Maybe if I read something it would take my mind off of all of the things I was thinking and feeling. The magazine turned out to be a Pentecostal Evangelical Magazine and the first words I read were "Why are you so certain that I didn't do as I promised? You are just looking for outward signs. Don't you know I work in the heart and much of My work is in secret? Don't you trust Me to do as I have said? My promises are yea and amen!" I got so excited I almost leaped over a row of washing machines. I got a scrap of paper and wrote the words down (and I regretted later that I had not written down the date and more information from the magazine's cover).

As I was writing, an elderly couple came into the laundromat. After they put their clothes into the machine, they sat near me and before long we struck up a conversation. It turned out that they were Christians and we ended up praying together. They told me that during our prayers they sensed that I needed to be patient in whatever situation I was in and I needed to continue to wait on the Lord.

That night during my time alone with the Lord, He told me to look for a "meeting of the minds." I had absolutely no idea what that meant and it would be quite some time before I finally understood. I knew that the elderly couple was right; I needed to be patient. I knew that God was working in Chet and I knew that it would be a passing of time before "the thing hoped for" would be a thing seen.

Divine Appointment

It was the practice of our prayer group to divide up our teaching assignments at the beginning of each month. I was scheduled to teach on the last meeting of the month and I was grateful for all of the time I would have to prepare, and I even thanked the Lord for the way it was arranged. I was very surprised when He told me to do it immediately and have it completed before the next prayer meeting. I had the time, so I did what He told me to do: I worked on it right away and even took time to practice my delivery. It was a great feeling to be done three weeks in advance.

At the next meeting, the person who was scheduled for the teaching was unable to attend due to an illness. No one was prepared to fill in except me. I called Chet and he brought the teaching to me and I gave it that night. I was so glad that I had listened to the Lord and it showed me again that He has everything under control. Since I had done the teaching for the man who was ill, he would be doing my teaching at the end of the month. Actually, I thought that worked out great. It meant that I wouldn't have to prepare a teaching until the end of the following month.

Tuesday evening came, and he did a great job. I was smiling to myself as I thought of all the time I would have before it was my turn again. It is amazing how quickly a great plan can change. After the teaching and fellowship ended, we gathered in our small group for more prayer time. It was then I was told that since we had flip-flopped my teaching time, I would be giving the teaching on the following Tuesday. I almost fell over—it was absolutely the worst possible time. I was having company for the four days before the teaching and I knew that I would be extremely busy. I figured that since the Lord had given me my last talk three weeks in advance, He would have a plan for this time too. I did have a few days to prepare a teaching, so I prayed for guidance thinking that the Lord would tell me what I was to teach on. I thought He would answer me right away and I could have it all done before my company arrived.

Sometimes the Lord is very, very silent. Obviously, He wasn't concerned about my dilemma and He didn't appear to be in any hurry to help me out. I prayed for three solid days and no ideas of any kind came to me, not even a Scripture that impressed me enough to build upon. On the day my company was to arrive, I was getting a little worried. I knew that if I did not have the teaching done by supper time, I would not have another chance before the meeting. "Lord, please speak to me by four o'clock—that is all the time I have," I prayed.

It was exactly four o'clock when the Lord gave me a Scripture verse. I looked it up and almost fell over. It was Luke 12:12, and it read: "The Holy Spirit will give you the right words even as you are standing there." My first concern was that I would stand up on Tuesday night and draw a blank. I knew that I'd have to keep on praying and that I would have to keep on trusting.

The Lord did give me two more Scriptures that helped to put my mind at ease. The first one was Isaiah 49:23: "Thou shalt know that I am the Lord, for they shall not be ashamed that wait for me." The second was Proverbs 3:5-6: "Trust in the Lord with all thy heart and lean not unto thine own understanding, in all ways acknowledge Him, and He shall direct thy paths."

I had a phone conversation with a friend of mine and he prayed with me. He told me that he would keep me in his prayers over the next few days. Then he said a strange thing. "You know, maybe this is the last teaching the Lord would have you do in this group." What made this even stranger was the fact that all the while I was waiting for the Lord to give me insight for my teaching, I had the same impression. I prayed that I would be open to the Holy Spirit and that I would not doubt but continue trusting the Lord.

Our company was easy to entertain, and even though the four days were filled with so many activities, we really had a great time. We were all so glad that we had been able to get together. Shortly after they left, Chet came home with news that I didn't expect. "What would you think about another move? They told me today that I was being transferred to Shakopee."

"Just a minute," I said. I ran into the office and shut the door. "All I want is a quick word, Lord, so I can answer Chet." I picked up the devotional that I had put on the chair (*Progress of Another Pilgrim*) and read, "Recognize My hand in this. It is truly by divine appointment. You can accept it knowing I will be in it." [9] A tremendous peace came over me and I knew the message was directly from the Lord. I came out of the office and told Chet what the Lord had just shown me. He said, "Well, then, I guess it's settled. We're moving to the cities."

The Lord had been so clear about our move from Cherry to Brainerd. He prepared me for it and told me about it even before Chet had a chance to tell me. I had a feeling that this time, everything would be quite different.

On Tuesday evening, I stood in front of my prayer group to give the teaching. My heart began to burn within me as I heard the words of the Holy Spirit speaking through me. The teaching was entirely on "Waiting on God." I was overwhelmed by the whole experience. Scripture verses were popping into my head and I was opening the Bible and turning the pages from one passage to another on waiting on God. God had proved faithful once again and I was in awe of how He had worked. Later, I was blessed again as I read II Peter 1:21, "Holy men of God spoke as they were moved by the Holy Spirit."

God Always Plans Ahead

Whenever I could, I attended a Thursday morning Bible study. During the winter it was held in Brainerd, but in the summer months the study met at Gull Lake, one of the many beautiful spots in the area. The pastor who led the study always centered his lessons on the Word of God, and his teachings were excellent. I was not as faithful in my attendance in the summer because the boys were out of school and it was often difficult to get a sitter. When I learned that we would be moving, I realized that I would not have many more chances to participate and I prayed asking God to provide a way.

One day one of my friends called and said that she would be going to the study and hoped that I could go with her. The kids happened to be gone all morning and I was delighted to accept her invitation. We had been friends for quite a while and had many great times together. We would be meeting her mom and sister-in-law at the lake and I was happy for the chance to see them again.

When we arrived, there were about nine women already sitting around the tables, each with their Bibles, all set to begin. My friend and I looked at them and realized that we didn't know any of them. Soon, her mom came and she too was surprised. Who were these women, and where were all of the regulars? And, where in the world was the Pastor? He always made it a practice to get there before anyone else so he could welcome us all and visit a little before beginning. We sat at the table watching the doors thinking that the others would be coming at any moment, but no one did.

Finally, one woman who was sitting at the table across from me, pointed at me and said very loudly, "You will lead this study today!" I turned to the others at my table and found them sitting with their heads bowed, ready for prayer. *Good grief, Lord, what's going on?* I opened my mouth to pray and at the same time, my heart was crying out to God with an SOS message. I knew that the prayer couldn't go on forever, so I asked the Lord what He wanted me to do. I opened the Bible to John 11. While the women took turns reading the chapter out loud, I prayed that God would give me the words He wanted me to share with them.

Suddenly, I was calm and I could feel the Lord's peace about me. He began to give me the message that He wanted these women to hear. The teaching was based on John 11:44 when Jesus called Lazarus forth from the tomb. "And Lazarus came, bound up in the gravecloth, his face muffled in a head swath." Jesus showed us how we too are like Lazarus, we are dead (in sin) but when we receive Christ into our lives, it is a new birth—we pass from death to life, but we come as Lazarus did, still wrapped up in our "grave clothes." Lazarus had to be unbound, and so do we. The Holy Spirit begins to work in us, and as we yield to Him He begins to show us areas that need changing—worldly things that bind us up. God doesn't deal with everything all at once, but as each area of our lives is changed our grave clothes are unwrapped. It can be a long process and sometimes we can get tangled up again in the things that we shouldn't, and they begin to trip us up. The Lord also brought to mind many Scriptures from the recent "Waiting on God" teaching at the prayer group and I shared them too. I marveled at how the Holy Spirit blended the two messages into an effective teaching. I can't remember everything I shared, but I knew that the Lord was able to use me that day.

The women thanked me and several shared that the Lord had touched them in a special way. One woman said that He really used the teaching to shed light on a situation that she had been dealing with for quite a while. Another woman was crying, and one was just standing there with a thoughtful expression on her face. I looked at my friend. She looked at me and said, "I cannot believe it." I knew what she meant, I couldn't get over the whole morning either. We had absolutely no idea what happened to the pastor or the regular Bible study and we did not know where these women had come from. One thing was obvious to us, and that was that the Lord had set this all up and taken care of every detail.

The woman who had pointed to me to say that I was to lead the study came over to my friend and I. She told us that she and the several of the others were vacationing at the lake. They were from the Twin Cities and would be returning there in a couple of days. When they heard there was a Bible study, they wanted to come. A few of the other women were vacationing at the lake and would be returning to the Twin Cities in a couple of days. They, too, wanted to come when they heard there was a

Bible study. The rest of the women lived in the area, and shared that they felt a strong desire to come that morning. The lady who was crying said that she felt led to come and just had to. It was really something. I was overwhelmed by the entire episode and couldn't wait until I could talk to the Lord about it.

The next morning, my friend called to tell me that she found out why the Bible study had been called. The Pastor and the person who usually filled in for him had other commitments and were unable to come. They decided it was best to just cancel the study. They informed everyone who attended on a regular basis, but forgot to let the women who came from Brainerd know.

I believe that Jesus planned everything and brought together the women He wanted to speak to. When I think back to that day, I just shake my head. It is so amazing to be a part of what God is doing—that morning was a miracle morning and it confirmed once again that God is in control.

"For His eyes are on the ways of a man, and He sees all of his steps." Job 34:21

"Wait on the Lord, be of good courage"
Psalm 27:14

It was the end of August, 1978, when we found out that we would be moving, and neither Chet nor I knew just how fast our move from Brainerd would be. By the second week in October we were in our new home in Shakopee.

When we moved from Cherry to Brainerd, God had made it so plain—everything was planned ahead of time, and the Lord was so gracious, speaking openly to me about all that would occur, taking care of every detail, and revealing the move step by step.

The move from Brainerd to Shakopee was a very different experience. Our first years in Shakopee were years of waiting on God, trusting in His provision, and leaning on Him for strength and support. They were also years of spiritual growth and a time of learning. The Holy Spirit is quite a teacher, and the lessons are forever burned in me.

One thing that really impressed me at this time was the chapter on faith in Hebrews 11. God was showing me that I would have to trust Him and have faith that He would bring everything into focus. Hadn't He proven faithful in the past? Hadn't He shown me that I could rely on Him in all things and trust Him to take care of us? Now, would I be able to trust Him completely even though I couldn't see clearly, even if He didn't give me any insight ahead of time? I thought I could; I knew I could—but I did not anticipate how difficult that would be.

A few weeks before moving, we had trouble with the septic tank and discovered that it would have to be fixed before we could sell the house. When the ground was dug up it revealed that the septic tank had been put in incorrectly and we would have to put in a whole new system. No one wanted to take responsibility for the faulty system—the contractor, the city inspector, the sub-contractors who completed the job following the final inspection—all were blaming each other. We spoke to a lawyer who informed us that in order to pursue this issue, we would have to contend with the city as well as everyone else that had a part in the procedure.

This was a time of serious prayer and we finally decided that we would pay to have a new system installed. The cost was more than we wanted to put out and it took most of the money that we had planned to use for our move. The fact that it was not our fault made the situation even harder. It seemed unjust that we would have to assume responsibility for someone else's error, but after speaking to the lawyer, we felt it was the best way to respond to the problem. A Scripture that the Lord gave me confirmed that this was the right decision. I Corinthians 6:7 says, "To have such lawsuits at all is a real defeat for you as a Christian. Why not just accept mistreatment and leave it at that. It would be far more honoring to the Lord to let yourselves be cheated." The peace was tremendous after accepting God's way and I knew in my heart that God would handle this. My only part would be to lift up those involved to God, forgive them, and pray for their salvation.

At the same time we were dealing with the septic situation, we had our closing date on the Shakopee house changed and we had to redo all of the things that had been pre-arranged. The bankers, the movers, the Realtor in Shakopee, etc., all had to be contacted and informed about the new circumstances. Finally, everyone was able to agree on a date.

At last, it was moving day. It was gray and cold and both boys woke up feeling crummy. I dismissed it as "moving blues" and we all went on with the final job of gathering the last few things together and loading them into the car. As soon as we were on our way, I opened to an entry from *On the High Road of Surrender.* I read "Go in joy and confidence, knowing that I go with you, and as you go, I enable you to walk in My grace." [10]

When we came to our new home, the Realtor informed us that we couldn't move into the house because the man who was to complete the final inspection had been unable to do it at the scheduled time, but had promised to try to get to our house later that day. In addition, the builder was not through with the kitchen—his wife was just finishing the final coat of varnish on the cabinets, and all of the appliances were sitting unconnected in the middle of the room. Everything was a mess—the basement was full of garbage that had accumulated during the building process, and to top it off, the movers were already in the driveway preparing to unload. We asked if they could delay a while until the inspector could get there, but they had another appointment scheduled and had to unload everything immediately. They did say they were sorry, then added that they didn't think of how cold the day would be when they loaded our belongings in the morning so all of the plants they put in the moving truck were frozen and ready for the garbage.

Everyone was a little testy—actually, Chet had passed testy and was bordering on furious. By this time, the boys' "crummy" feeling from the early morning had turned into something more serious. They were both running a temperature and complaining about their ears hurting. In addition, my mom was arriving by bus in a little while and we would have to find out where the bus depot was so we could pick her up. I had already sent up a prayer for her; I knew she would be expecting the same situation we had when we moved to Brainerd, and she would be in for quite a shock when she arrived to find chaos.

I prayed for the boys to feel better, for comfort for Chet as he dealt with all of the events, and peace for me. As I prayed, I began to see things in the Spirit. I knew we had arrived right on time and it was God's will. Satan was working overtime to discourage us and to make everything look like a giant mistake. The more he tried to interfere and upset us, the more I felt at peace knowing how much God wanted us here. As the day wore on, I thought many times what God had told me earlier—that this is by "divine appointment."

Fortunately, the builder and his wife were sympathetic. They saw our dilemma and said that the movers could put the furniture and all of our other belongings into the house. I was able to get a doctor to see the boys and he confirmed that they both had ear infections and needed medication. My mom arrived and did fine with everything that was going on. The inspector finally came, and we were able to get into the house by the end of the day.

I could see that this move was bringing with it a whole new dimension in my walk with the Lord, and I had to rely on Romans 28 more than once: "And we know that all things work together for good to them that love God, to them who are called according to His purpose." And Hebrews 13:5: "I will never leave thee, nor forsake thee."

The move to Shakopee was a big move financially for us, and even with the help that Chet's company gave us in securing financing for the house and handling moving expenses, we were in a bind. This house was much smaller than the one we had just left, it was only partially finished, there was no driveway and the yard was just a pile of dirt. Even so, the house was more expensive, and our monthly payments had almost doubled. We did not go overboard in our selection of houses, yet we couldn't believe how unrealistic housing costs were. As a matter of fact, several people made the amusing comment that for what we paid for the house, they were surprised that we even had running water and lights.

One more event threw us for a loop—when we had been in Cherry and then Brainerd, Chet had been provided with a company car. He was told that he would be able to use it in Shakopee until the end of the year. We were in Shakopee less than a week when they said they needed the car back. There were still bills from Brainerd—the septic tank, draperies, medical and dental responsibilities, etc., all had to be taken care of—and now, to top it off, we had to add a car payment. The move had happened so quickly that we didn't have time to meet old obligations before we added new ones. We began our very first day with the clinic bill for the boys' ear infections. Plus, we contracted for the driveway before we knew about the car, and workers had already started on that project.

One good thing—Chet had been promised a nice increase with his transfer. That along with several other promises made by company representatives left us confident that help was on the way. Shortly after he started working in the new office, he was told by his boss that there would be a delay with any pay increase. In truth, neither the pay raise or a single one of the other promises made to Chet ever materialized. We found ourselves with higher payments, less income, and growing financial commitments. We felt as if we were in a battle and each day presented a new struggle. "Consider it pure joy, my brothers, whenever you face trials of many kinds, because you know that the testing of your faith develops perseverance." (James 1:2-3)

How grateful I am that I am a child of God. I have the assurance that no matter what the circumstances might be, no matter what problems arise, He is right beside me. The Lord's provision during all of this was beyond our expectations and we lived a "miracle existence" from month to month.

"How gracious He will be when you cry for help! As soon as He hears, He will answer you." Isaiah 30:19

"A righteous man may have many troubles, but the Lord delivers him from them all." Psalm 34:19

> **"By this shall all men know that you are my disciples,**
> **If you have love for one another."**
> **John 13:35**

SOS, Lord! I need prayer support. I need a Christian friend—some kind of contact with a believer!

Chet and I were on our way to the post office when I said out loud, "Lord, do something, I could sure use a touch by another Christian!" Chet just gave me one of those sideways glances and shook his head. A few minutes later, he came out of the post office and handed me a letter. It was a letter from a friend, and it was filled with praises to God. She had been praying for a deeper walk with the Lord and had recently received the Baptism in the Holy Spirit. God had been doing all sorts of things in her life and she couldn't help but rejoice and praise Him. I rejoiced myself as I read her letter. God knew how badly I needed to receive such good news.

As great a blessing as it was, it still did not meet my need for fellowship. I remembered the way I felt in Brainerd and how God brought so many wonderful people into my life. I knew He had something in store for me here too.

One afternoon Chet called to tell me that there was going to be a birthday party for one of the people he worked with, and that the wives were invited to attend. I hadn't met a single person that Chet was working with at this time, so I was a little uncomfortable about going. On the day of the party, I prayed that the Lord would send someone that I could talk to. As soon as we arrived at the party, Chet introduced me around, then he began "talking shop" to one of the salesmen. I found an empty chair against the wall and sat down.

I noticed a man and woman enter the room, and I could tell by the expression on her face that she didn't know anyone there either. She took the seat next to me and at once I felt close to her. Not just physically because we were seated next to one another, but spiritually close. I had a warm, comfortable feeling come over me and I knew the Lord had brought us together. We struck up a conversation and I could tell instantly that I liked this person—Cleo's eyes just danced when she spoke. We were about three minutes into our conversation when the subject turned to Jesus. Everything we shared was so fantastic that I almost wanted to shout, and she said that she felt the same way. Before long, the two of us had a prayer meeting right there! It was wonderful—not a single person interrupted us and we had the opportunity to get to know each other better.

Cleo attended a Bible study in Prior Lake—just a short drive from Shakopee, and when she invited me to join her, I eagerly accepted. The Bible study was an uplifting experience, and just what I needed. I looked forward to attending each week, but I still longed for a Christian friend in Shakopee.

One afternoon, I received a call from a woman named Bev. Bev was from Shakopee and attended a Bible study on Thursday mornings. She had been visiting the local hospital and met one of the women who was in the Prior Lake study. She obtained my phone number from her and decided to call me right away. We talked for a long time and then arranged a coffee date to continue our visit. I began to attend Bible study with her and met more wonderful sisters in the Lord.

During the first few weeks in Shakopee, I did not attend any church services. There was an Assemblies of God church a block from our house—very convenient, but the Lord hadn't given me any word about going there. I decided that since the Lord had me in the Catholic church in Brainerd, that I would attend a Catholic church here. The first service I went to turned out to be an awful experience. I smiled at several people and said "Hello," but no one responded with so much as a nod. It bothered me, but it was a Saturday evening service, it was a cold night, and I just thought that everyone was in a hurry to get in and out again. I came home feeling like I hadn't even been to church. The next week I went and it was the same. For a moment, I thought that I might be invisible—even the people I sat next to or brushed up against when I walked in didn't seem to see me. Finally, one of the Deacons actually looked at me and smiled. "Speak to that man about a prayer meeting," the Lord told me. After the service was over, I saw him standing by the door. I went up to him and introduced myself. I asked him if he knew of any prayer groups that might be meeting in the area. It turned out that there was, and that they were held on Sunday evenings at the church. They were just about to begin a Life in the Spirit seminar, and the Deacon suggested I come.

I was happy for the opportunity to go to my first meeting, but I did not expect to feel so incredibly uneasy—very few people were talking, and when anyone came by me, they spoke only briefly. One couple there was more open and we did spend time in conversation—they invited me to attend a Charismatic conference with them the following week and I accepted their invitation.

Later, during my prayer time, the Lord impressed upon me that He would use me in the group. The Scripture verse that kept coming to me was Acts 18:9: "Speak out, don't be afraid, don't quit! For I am with you, and no one can harm you. Many in this city belong to Me. So Paul stayed the next year and a half teaching the truths of God." As it turned out, it would be quite some time before I would be involved in any way.

I continued to go to mass for a couple of months, and in that entire time, no one except for that deacon even said hello. It really was difficult for me to understand—I tried to be friendly, but to no avail. It was a terrible time, and I spoke to the Lord about it, asking Him for guidance and wisdom. Some of the people who were in the prayer group were members there, but in all the time I went, I never saw a single one of them. The deacon was never there again either, so I couldn't even count on him for another smile.

Days of prayer brought no word from the Lord. I no longer felt comfortable in the Catholic church, but had no leading to leave. Besides, I had met a number of Catholic Christians and their desire was to remain in the church and witness to as many people as they could. I wanted God to give me a clear vision of what He wanted me to do.

Slowly, the Lord began to speak to me. First, He told me to look deeply into my heart. He showed how my belief in many of the things that I had been taught as a child had changed since I committed my life to Him. I had already stopped saying the rosary, and I found no scriptural support for a number of other practices in the church—the strong devotion to Mary and the saints, her assumption into Heaven, her sinlessness, the doctrine of Purgatory, etc., were just some of them.

Two of the biggest issues for me were the teaching of the "sacrifice of the mass" as if Jesus is nailed afresh to the cross at each service, and the communion service that taught that the bread and wine were actually receiving the body and blood of Jesus rather than something done in "remembrance".

The next thing the Lord impressed upon me was that even though I had come to terms with these things, I was still clinging to them—I needed to let go, once and for all, of the things I once believed. I was no longer enslaved to any of them and I needed to stand in my freedom. The Lord told me that I must not stand alone and I needed communion with those "like-minded." I knew that He meant beyond the Bible studies and the prayer group. He told me not to let anything hinder me, and that I was not to please men—I was to please Him. There would be people in my life who would not understand this, especially members of my family. I knew that some of them would take it personally, but I knew what the Lord was telling me, and I wanted to please Him above all. Jesus told me to be obedient and to loose myself from my present bondage. He confirmed what He told me through several inspirational messages, and I knew that the Catholic church would no longer be part of my life. For the first time in weeks, I had a deep peace.

There was no more questioning the Lord about this matter. He made it clear what I was to do. I believe He permitted the people at mass to not see me, and the rejection I felt was necessary to bring me to this point in my life. In contrast, He made the reception I received the first time I went to the Shakopee Assemblies of God church warm, welcoming, and extremely pleasant. I began attend services on a regular basis and I knew that I would remain there until the Lord told me differently. I wanted to begin to go to the Sunday evening services too, but Jesus made it clear that even though I was to leave the Catholic church, I was to remain in the Catholic Charismatic prayer group. I was somewhat puzzled until He reminded me that He still had a work for me to do and the time to leave would come soon enough.

This prayer group was so different from others I had attended. The other groups were open and friendly; everyone was eager to share the Lord and what He was doing in their lives. The feeling of belonging, warmth, and friendship permeated the atmosphere. Not so in this group. For a long time I felt more like an outsider than a member—rather than being welcomed to the group, there was a sense that you had to "earn your way." I didn't understand God's reasoning, and more than once I asked Him to let me leave. His answer was always no. I thought that it would be easier each time I went, but it wasn't. There were truly some remarkable Christians in the group who were helpful and friendly, but my vision was clouded by the few who displayed a cold and unwelcoming face.

I had been in the prayer group for quite some time when the Lord began to speak to me about being a part of the teaching ministry. Fat chance, Lord. I really thought that it was impossible. On one or two occasions when the whole group would share, I would participate, but teaching was something else. I began to pray earnestly about it. I knew that the idea could not come from me, but had to come from the leadership. One Sunday, after we had finished a seminar, we met to discuss the different ministries. A sheet of paper was passed around that had a list of all the ministries. On the bottom were directions to check those we were most interested in and a space to write our experiences in this area. I thought over the things the Lord had been saying to me and especially the words I had read that afternoon. They were from a book called *Progress of Another Pilgrim* and read:

> "My people need direction, they need to hear a clear voice giving them the wisdom of God. Be not negligent concerning the gift I have given you. Do not allow it to become dormant. I have given it to you knowing the full urgency of this hour. Be up and about your Father's business. Let nothing else claim priority over this, My commission for you. Give yourself to a life of prayer and much careful study of the Word that you may be able to give My message with clarity and the unction of the Holy Spirit. Lo, the message is mine, but I have need of those who will speak out and who will give it faithfully without alteration and without any attempt to please men." [11]

I checked the box next to the words "teaching ministry," and wrote a few words referring to the involvement I'd had in my previous prayer group. Throughout the next week, I prayed about this and the Lord continued to impress upon me that this was His will for me in this group. The following Sunday evening, I was approached by the leadership team and they told me that it would be impossible for me to participate in the teaching ministry. They made it clear that I would have to "prove myself." I shared some of the Scriptures and messages that the Lord led me to and the way He had spoken to me. They said that they could not accept me in the ministry based on those things alone. They would be the ones to select the appropriate ministry for me and told me then to sign up to work in the kitchen. I had served in just about every ministry at one time or another, but it was always by the Lord's leading. They told me to come to a special ministries meeting on Thursday evening and they would explain the duties to me. When I got home, I prayed for a long time, and listened to the still small voice within. The Lord told me that I was not to allow man to lead me to a place of compromise—"I have already told you what to do, Mary, and you must do it."

I met that Thursday with the leadership and others who had signed up for various ministries. The people in charge of the kitchen ministry said that they'd been given my name, but had no need for me; they had more than enough help already. In fact, there was no room left in any of the ministries. Why in the world had the Lord brought me into this group? Had I misunderstood what He was telling me? In the past, He had always given several others the same words He gave me, and always confirmed everything so there was never doubt or confusion. Why, this time, when His guidance was so clear to me, hadn't He spoken to anyone else?

I left the meeting feeling a little puzzled about the outcome. I spent over an hour praying and asking the Lord to help me understand what was going on. His word to me was clear—I was certain that I hadn't misunderstood, but the coolness the leadership team displayed, and their unwillingness to talk to me, left me wondering what to do next. I felt the Lord saying that I should not grow tired, or become involved in self-pity. Just before I ended my time with the Lord, I read the following words in *Come Away My Beloved*: "Behold, My hand is upon thee to bless thee and to accomplish all My good purpose, for this hour, I have prepared thy heart, and in My kindness, I will not let thee fail." [12] I had the assurance that when it came time for me to do any teaching or more in-depth sharing, God would make it possible and no one would stand in His way.

The Lord began to work on me over the next days. He revealed that my attitude had not been right and the feelings that I had been harboring had to be dealt with. I didn't want to accept the different way this group conducted things—I liked the ways that I was used to. I saw that I had been unbending and unwilling to make changes. Some of the changes would eventually work themselves out as I matured in the Lord; others would have to be dealt with right away. God also showed me that He was working in the group and was bringing them into a deeper walk and better understanding of things concerning them. I had been so involved with my own feelings that I overlooked the way the Lord was working in the others. I had felt the rejection of so many in the group, yet, the Lord revealed to me my reluctance to accept them because they were not what I had expected them to be. I wanted my transition from the Brainerd group to be a sideways move so things could just continue on in the comfortable fashion I had come to enjoy. This was different, and I lost my perspective—I wanted to cling to the old ways, and had allowed my feelings and thoughts to blow things out of proportion. As the Lord began to reveal these things to me, I began to confess the attitudes I had allowed to develop, and I renewed my commitment to do what God wanted me to do.

Once I was willing to "let go and let God" deal with me, I felt free and at peace. When the Lord had told me that "this hour I have prepared thy heart" I finally knew what He meant. He now had me in a position where He could again use me and work through me. At the same time that all of this was happening, God taught me two more important lessons: first, in all of our difficulties we are to look for reasons to be thankful, and second, God will use all of the circumstances in our lives to shape us into the person He wants us to be. Two Scriptures really spoke to my heart at this time.

"After you have suffered a little while, our God, who is full of kindness through Christ, will give you His eternal glory. He personally will come and pick you up, and set you firmly in place, and make you stronger than ever." I Peter 5:10

"Now you can have real love for everyone because your souls have been cleansed from selfishness and hatred when you trusted Christ to save you; so see to it that you really do love each other warmly with all your hearts." I Peter 1:22

The Egyptian Mouse

God used a practical lesson to illustrate further truth to me concerning my involvement with the prayer group. It helped me to see that we can lose our direction in our desire to have things remain as they once had been.

One morning after Chet had left for work and the boys had gone off to school, I went into the laundry room to do a load of wash. I looked into the laundry tub and saw a fat little gray mouse. My heart just about stopped! I got my bearings and realized that the little guy was trapped—and at that particular moment was experiencing far more trauma than I was. It was evident that he had fallen into the tub during the night. He was probably scurrying around in the dark, running along the edge of the tub, unaware of the impending danger, then suddenly falling. I could tell how frantic he was and how hard he must have worked to get up the slippery smooth walls. He appeared helpless, frightened and totally exhausted. Well, I wasn't quite certain what to do. One thing I was sure of—I wasn't going to spend an entire day with a mouse in the laundry room.

I looked out of the window and saw that my neighbor was still at home, so I called and asked if he would come over and get the mouse out of the tub. He came immediately, with a big glove on his hand, and proceeded to pick up the mouse. He walked toward the patio door, mouse in hand, and was just about to open it when I asked, "Aren't you going to kill it?"—hoping he would say yes and no at the same time. "No," he replied, "I haven't got the heart. I'll just let him go." He put him outside and closed the patio door.

The two of us looked out of the glass and witnessed a most remarkable event. The mouse just stood there. Then it did a very strange thing. It looked at the empty field ahead, and then looked back at the house, gazing at us—then in just a flash of time, it did the same thing again. It was almost as if it was making a decision as to what to do next. To my dismay, it ran back toward the house. *How stupid,* I thought. I set a trap, and by evening, he had paid the consequences of his bad decision.

I couldn't get over the whole episode and mentioned to the Lord how it had affected me. "I can't imagine why that mouse ran back. It was free, yet it chose to return to the very place where it had faced danger the night before. I'm sure glad I'm not that way, Lord. I just can't get over the stupidity of that mouse!"

The Lord impressed me with an unexpected explanation of what I had witnessed. I was reminded of the parables He used when He taught the disciples and crowds who followed Him. When the disciples questioned Him, He always made the meaning clear, and He did the same for me.

"The mouse is like My children often are. They are in bondage, trapped with no way of escape. I provide a way to freedom, but even when they are standing in liberty, they long for the times of slavery with all of the fleshy comforts." In spite of the dangers and chance of death, my house provided the mouse with shelter, warmth, and food, just like God's people in Egypt experienced along with the abuse and slavery. Out in the elements, even though the mouse had freedom, it would have to be responsible and disciplined to face that freedom. God's people faced hardships and trials, they didn't want to be disciplined. They desired the things that the world offered. The Lord showed me how I had gotten used to certain comforts—how "soft" I had grown and how easy I wanted thing to be. There is no growth in Egypt. Only out, facing the discipline of freedom, could God deal with me. He permitted me to feel the rejection and coolness of those in the prayer group. He allowed me to stand and make a choice like that mouse—looking back at what was, or looking ahead to the new things He had planned for me.

I wanted to move forward with the Lord and my heart was at peace with that decision. Even if I didn't have the comfortable, easy feeling I had in my other prayer groups, I knew that walking close to the Lord was the most important thing for me. The Lord dealt with me in a very personal way, and I doubted if anyone in the group ever sensed what I had been going through. "So Christ has made us free—now, make sure you stay free!" (Galatians 5:1a); "So if the Son sets you free, you shall be free indeed." (John 8:36)

Jesus is the one who sets us free—freedom from sin, bondage self-centeredness, etc. After this experience and all the Lord had been doing in my heart, I was finally at a point where I could be free to attend the prayer meetings with no strings attached. The Lord opened the doors for me to enjoy a wonderful fellowship—I no longer felt rejected and shut out, instead, I felt part of God's family again. And, in His good time, He opened the doors for me to be involved with the teaching ministry.

Once I accepted the situation in the Shakopee group and stopped comparing it to what I had been involved in, and once I was willing to move on in the Lord and not cling to the things that used to be, God was able to work in me. I was thankful for all I had experienced and knew that whatever was to come, He would see me through.

Water Baptism

When I was a little girl, I had a desire in my heart that I never shared with anyone. One of my favorite Bible stories that I heard in catechism class was the story of Jesus and how He was baptized by John the Baptist. I could close my eyes and imagine Jesus stepping into the water and standing in front of John. I could see the sunlight streaming down on him as the Heavens opened and God spoke. I wanted to be baptized just like this too, but it wasn't a practice in the Catholic church and I thought that my parents wouldn't understand if I told them how I felt. I knew of no one, except for Jesus, who had been baptized like this, and even though I heard that some churches believe in this kind of baptism, I knew no one personally who had experienced it.

After becoming a Christian, I had an even stronger desire to experience water baptism. One Sunday morning shortly after I had started attending services at the Assemblies of God, the Pastor announced that there were several new converts who would be going to an Assemblies of God church nearby to be baptized by immersion. He asked all who had not been baptized in this way to join them. This was something that I had wanted for so long, and now I finally had the opportunity to do it. "Each one of you must turn from sin, return to God, and be baptized in the name of Jesus for the forgiveness of your sins; then you also shall receive this gift, the Holy Spirit." Acts 2:38

I knew that I had salvation through Jesus Christ, that I was a born-again believer; I also knew that Jesus had baptized me in the Holy Spirit. I know that there is no "saving power" in the water, our sins can only be washed away by the blood, but baptism is a mark of obedience. Sin's power was broken when I became a Christian, and being baptized by immersion meant for me the death to the old nature forever. Drowning the things of the old life, and rising into the newness of life. When I came up out of that water, I felt even more completely given over to God. It impressed upon me to a greater degree than ever before that I had passed from death to life, and I wanted God to be sovereign over every part of me and in every area of my life. "To be a tool in His hands, and to be used for His good purposes. Sin need never again be my master; no longer tied to the law where sin enslaves, but free under God's favor and mercy." (Romans 6:13-14)

Following the baptism experience, I felt that there was a change in the way I looked at things. Prior to that time, I saw things more as hind sight. After each experience, I could look back and see how the Lord had worked in my life. I saw how He dealt with me, how He engineered circumstances in my behalf, and how He taught me the lessons I needed to learn. That still occurred, but I began to see Jesus at work more in the present.

One thing that happened illustrated this to me more clearly. I was walking in the back yard when I stepped into a small hole and twisted my ankle. I immediately saw that God had a purpose in it and began to praise and thank Him for what had happened to me. I limped into the house and took a better look at my ankle. It was pounding with pain and had doubled in size; still, I felt very peaceful about it.

I picked up my Bible and opened it to Hosea 6 and read, "Let us return to the Lord; it is He who has torn us and He will heal us, He has wounded and He will bind us up. In just a couple of days, or three at the most, He will set us on our feet again." The Lord then impressed me to call an acquaintance for prayer. Normally, I would have called someone from my Bible study or prayer group, but this time, I didn't. The feeling to call one specific person was so strong, that I called her. When she answered the phone, she was in great distress. She poured out her problem to me and I began to pray with her. It was only at the end of the conversation that I remembered to ask her for prayer for my ankle. Suddenly, my need had become so small—hers was the greater.

I saw several things—first, had I not sprained my ankle, I never would have made the phone call. Second, had I not experienced pain myself, I could not have appreciated someone else's pain. Third, had I not recognized God in the entire situation, I would have maximized my own pain to the degree that I would not have had the opportunity to help someone with a greater pain. Just as the Scripture stated, on the third day I was totally healed. Suddenly, the pain disappeared, the swelling went down, and the ankle was normal again. So often we make our circumstances bigger than life. We act as though we are the only ones suffering. Only our desires and needs seem important, but in truth, there are many who have needs greater and more urgent than our own.

God showed me that there are many ways to handle the things that come into our lives. At one time I would have had a pity party for myself. I would have wanted the attention and sympathy of others. I would not have praised God or turned to Scripture—in fact, the reverse would have occurred; I would have grumbled and asked, "Why me?" I would have been miserable because of my attitude and the choice I had made to focus on myself. When I began to get my focus on the Lord, I began to see His hand on every moment of my day, not just when I prayed, or when I "came through" various circumstances.

The things I learned from my ankle experience began with a physical pain, but some of the lessons I learned began with a heart pain.

> **"Anger is cruel, and fury overwhelming,
> but who can stand before jealousy?"
> Proverbs 27:4**

It was the night of Chet's 20th class reunion. Everyone was engaged in lively conversation as they reminisced and brought each other up to date. One of the people who sat at our table was a woman that Chet had dated in high school. I had never thought about the dates that Chet and I had before we met; that all seemed like a light year ago. I knew he held no interest in anyone else, and I was certain he knew that I had no interest in another person either.

Throughout the evening, this woman seemed to be paying a great deal of attention to Chet. At first, I thought it was my imagination, but no matter where he went, she kept searching him out. Whenever I turned around they would be standing off by themselves deep in conversation. You know what it's like at a reunion—everyone is everywhere, couples separate as they walk around to visit with old friends and renew old acquaintances. Chet and I were separated dozens of times that night, and each time when I discovered where he was stationed, there at his side was this woman. I couldn't figure out why this person was so bent on cornering Chet (I gave him the benefit of the doubt and didn't accuse him of seeking her out). I no longer thought I was imagining this attraction, and several people who had also observed what was taking place were very anxious to bring it to my attention.

People were visiting or dancing, and I found myself sitting alone. As I watched everyone, the happy peace I'd had at the onset of the evening began to fade. With each passing minute, I felt more anxious and upset. This was from the pit, and the pit director was not about to let me get by with a minor agitation; no, instead, he began to whisper—"Look, Chet looks interested in her. He's smiling and laughing. He's not interested in where you are—no concern that you're all by yourself! Who knows, maybe he's the one cornering her? He hasn't been seeking you out, now has he?" On and on, thoughts like these were winding their way through my mind. I felt my cheeks flush and a sick feeling grow within my stomach. *Why,* I thought angrily, *I ought to march right over to the two of them and let them know just what I thought, confront them right on the spot.* After all, this wasn't my reunion—I wasn't the one who deserted my spouse and abandoned him at a table to sit alone! On and on these thoughts went. It didn't help to see this woman arm and arm with Chet in a far corner of the room. I could almost hear the devil say, "Just look at them! You have a right to be angry and hurt; why, you poor thing, and you came thinking you were going to have fun! You were so generous to let Chet visit with his classmates, and look how he turned on you."

By this time, my anger was at a boiling point and my self-pity was forming into a giant-sized party. "Oh, Lord," I said, "How can this be happening? The evening started out so nice, and now Chet spoiled everything. Lord," I continued, "I am so angry—I feel left out. I'd like to scream at both of them and tell them a thing or two. Look at her hanging on Chet's arm. He should be with me. I hate the attention he is giving her. He is spending all of his time with her while I sit here alone."

The Lord seemed less interested in what Chet was doing, and more interested in pointing out what I was doing. I felt His words move through my mind, "Mary, you sound jealous." I let the word sink in. I thought over the events of the evening...jealousy...that's what this is all about? I never thought I could be jealous of anyone or anything in my life, yet, as the Lord brought it to my attention, I could see that I was indeed jealous. Praise God! How could it have taken me so long to realize it? Satan really had me going there for a while. I was actually believing his lies. "Thank You, Lord for revealing my sin. I never knew I could be like that. Forgive me for my jealousy and my anger, envy and resentment. Forgive me for not trusting Chet and for allowing these feelings to get in the way of my thinking clearly. Thank You, Lord for guiding me through this. I'm trusting You for the rest of this evening. Upset stomach, sweaty palms, anger-flushed cheeks, jealousy—that's not my style, and it's not Your way either. Thank You for the peace I feel now." I felt renewed, refreshed and victorious. I was so glad that I listened to the Lord.

I decided to freshen my make-up and when I came back from the ladies room, I glanced around for Chet. He was still with the woman, but it was okay now. God had replaced my jealous feelings with the right attitude. I went over to them and said, "Hi, you two. Having fun?" The woman mumbled something and left. Chet looked at me for a moment, then he said, "I'm sure glad that I am with you. That one sure has a bad outlook on life. She's been grumbling and complaining and crying the blues to me all night. I feel sorry for her—she seemed so messed up and unhappy. I didn't know what to tell her, so I told her that maybe she should pray about it, and maybe talk to you instead of me." Chet looked at me again and asked, "Why are you grinning like that?"

I shared all that had been going on with me. How I had allowed the temptation of jealousy to hit me. How foolish I had acted, and how the Lord set me straight. "Hey, I'm curious. What if your suspicions were right? What if you came over and found out that it was just like you were thinking? I bet you would have clobbered me on the spot."

"No," I answered. "I realized something else tonight. I love you no matter what, and I'd forgive you. You are more important to me than anyone else and I'd fight to keep you and what we have together." Chet gave me a hug and we went in to join the others.

The music had started and we went onto the dance floor. We danced and hugged and just looked at each other the rest of the night. It must have been noticeable, because several people we knew started pointing at us. One of the guys even yelled out across the dance floor, "Hey, what's with the two of you? You look like you just fell in love!" When we came back to our table, several people were already sitting there. "You two are acting like newlyweds!" Chet and I just laughed.

Now, another thing happened—that beautiful feeling lasted for months. We couldn't even mention the reunion without grinning, and Chet was the worst! Every time we talked about it, he would grin and blush.

Everything that happened that night brought us closer and I could feel the Lord's smiling approval. He had definitely worked a work in me and on the two of us. It was terrific. It had taken a while that night for me to turn to the Lord and recognize the jealousy in my heart. Once it was out before the Lord, I believed I would never be confronted with it again.

As usual, I was mistaken.

Wonderful Debbie

Chet and I were in the habit of sharing the events of our day with one another. We were in such a conversation when Chet mentioned that one of the girls that worked in the company was being transferred to his department to assume the secretarial duties. He had talked to her on the phone many times, but had never met her in person.

In the days and weeks to follow, I had the feeling that perhaps Debbie should have remained just a voice on the phone. Her presence at work was obviously having an affect on Chet, and he never passed up an opportunity to tell me about "wonderful Debbie." Debbie did this, and Debbie did that—wonderful, perfect, efficient, nice Debbie. She's talented, types over 90 words a minute and is so organized. *YUCK!* I thought. I found myself not liking Debbie. As the weeks passed, I found myself not liking the fact that Chet liked Debbie and that he thought so much of her. He even had the boys all fired up about Debbie, and they couldn't wait to meet her. It wasn't long before they had the chance.

Debbie had invited several of the people from work and their families to spend a day at the lake with her family. She wanted everyone to come and take advantage of the sun, go swimming, fish and boat ride, or just relax and do whatever they wanted to do. But that weekend, Chet had been having problems with his ankles and near the end of the week they were swollen and causing a lot of pain. He had several sleepless nights and was having difficulty moving easily. *At least we won't be going to the lake with wonderful Debbie,* I thought. Then the weather turned rainy, and I was glad about that too.

You can imagine how surprised I was when Chet said we were not going to disappoint Debbie. We were going. I mentioned all the pain he was in, the crummy weather, and the long drive to the lake. "You should be going to the doctor, or spending the day in bed!" Nothing I said would sway him one bit. "Look," Chet told me, "Deb and her family have prepared a lot and it wouldn't be right not to go after we accepted. Besides with all this rain, she has to be feeling disappointed already." The whole matter was settled in his mind, so I decided to pray about it.

The Lord said only one word to me—"Go!" I prayed some more, and the Lord began to reveal that the spirit of jealousy over Debbie was causing me to lose my focus. I made the decision that I would not allow the sin of jealousy to surface and cause a problem. I recalled how the Lord had dealt with me before. God had given me victory then, and I knew that I could have victory now. I refused to fall into temptation again, and I took authority over it in Jesus' name. "Resist the devil, and he will flee from you!"

By the time we arrived at the lake, I was feeling better about the whole thing. Debbie and her family had gone through a lot of trouble making the preparations, and I know they must have been disappointed with the rain and the poor turnout. Debbie's family was so nice and made us feel welcome and comfortable. Her mother was a perfect hostess, and Debbie was everything Chet said she was. The boys were really captured by her—she catered to them and, when the weather cleared up, she took them out on the boat and spent her afternoon fishing and swimming with them. I discovered that I liked Debbie too. I could see that Chet's interest in her was almost like a fatherly attitude. I had a sense that something else was going to happen, but I couldn't put my finger on it. I thought of asking Chet if there was anything about Debbie that I should be aware of, but I never got around to it. One thing I did decide to do was to add Debbie to my prayer list.

One evening, Chet, the boys, and I were out shopping. I thought that it would be nice if we stopped for a coke or something, but Chet said no. He just wanted to get home. He was really tired, and it was a school night and the boys needed to be in bed soon. I agreed with him. We barely pulled out of the parking lot when Chet said, "Let's go to Debbie's." He obviously wasn't tired anymore, and the fact that it was already getting dark no longer seemed to be an issue either. The boys just went wild. I was confused over this quick change of plans, but I chose to just accept it. Debbie's apartment was nearby—I had only been there once when Chet and I and another person from work had helped her move.

The first thing I noticed was a book on Debbie's coffee table. The word "thin" was on the cover and attracted me immediately. I always battled the scale and was open to any insight on the subject of weight.

I picked up the book and pages through the first chapter. It contained a commitment prayer and Scripture verses—my heart just leaped within me. I asked Debbie if she read the book and she told me that she had wanted to but had been far too busy. When we got home, I mentioned the book and the Scripture references to Chet. His answer surprised me. "Can't you see—He is trying to reach Debbie through me, through you," he said as he pointed a finger toward the sky. I knew that the Holy Spirit had urged us to go to Debbie's home that night, and I continued to pray for her that God would draw her and that she would come into a relationship with Him.

One afternoon, I was praying when I heard the mail truck outside. Ordinarily, I don't stop during my prayer time. I usually even have the phone off the hook so I'm not disturbed, but this time, I had a strong urge to go out and get the mail. There was only one envelope, a card from Debbie. She sent us a lovely note thanking us for being so kind to her and for helping her move. She had enjoyed our visit, too. There were also four hockey tickets in the card. Now, I'm not really moved to tears over hockey tickets, but when I looked at Deb's signature, I began to sob. I could not stop. They were deep sobs that came from way inside of me and I began to pray for Debbie like I had never prayed before. I cried out to the Lord for her, praying in the Spirit, and claiming her for the Kingdom of Christ. It went on for a long time, and the praying overwhelmed me. I felt the presence of the Holy Spirit in a powerful way. When I finished praying, a deep feeling of peace washed over me.

The next day, Debbie called to see if Chet could look at her car. She had been having trouble with it and didn't know what the problem was. While Chet worked on the car, Deb and I visited. We covered several general topics and then got into a discussion on our mutual weight problem. Deb had lost a lot of weight, and was working hard to maintain. I, on the other hand, had made a number of trips up and down the scale and was presently on the up side of things. I asked her if she would like to pray together about our weight. When she said yes, I was relieved. I didn't know what her response would be, and when she agreed, I was glad that I had asked.

We went into the bedroom for more privacy, and I sat on the bed. Deb knelt on the floor. "You pray," she said. I just simply asked God to give us strength and direction where our weight was concerned. I could tell that this was something that Deb wasn't used to and I didn't want to get too lengthy. I looked at Debbie. She had her head down, she was crying, and I could see her shoulders shaking and her hands trembling. "Now, Mary, tell her about Me." I told Debbie about Jesus' love and how He understands our deepest longings and greatest needs. I went through several Scriptures and asked Deb if she had ever invited Jesus into her life. She shook her head and said that she really wanted to but didn't know how.

I shared the salvation message with Deb and prayed a commitment prayer. She prayed along with me and began her walk with the King of Kings. Nothing can describe that moment. For me, it was awesome to see the Holy Spirit at work and a privilege to be used as His instrument. I can't tell you what Debbie was feeling, but I knew that she would never be the same again. I have since seen her grow into a mature Christian, more in love with Jesus than ever before. Debbie began to attend prayer meetings and read the Bible more frequently, and we prayed together whenever we had the chance. Her new relationship with the Lord had brought us closer. Our family would be facing some difficult days and the Lord had put Debbie in a position to be a strong support and a prayer warrior on our behalf.

The Potter's Hand

It is difficult to write all of the things that happened during our first years in Shakopee. So many of the experiences overlap or are related to each other in some way. How to separate them and still pull them together is quite a task, and I have to wait on the Lord, relying on the Holy Spirit to steer me in the right direction. One of the hardest to write about concerns our oldest son, Tony.

I need to turn the clock back a few years to tell the complete story. Tony was about four years old when he began to have bladder infections. They occurred frequently, and at the suggestion of our pediatrician, we had x-rays taken. They revealed that Tony had only one kidney and it was located in the pelvic area where it rested on the pelvic bone.

We learned this before I committed my life to Christ, and I did not know a powerful loving God to turn to. Oh, I prayed, but my prayers seemed to hit the ceiling and bounce back at me. Every time I thought about Tony, I imagined all kinds of wild things happening to him. I just ached for him and this thing we had discovered. The doctor assured us that although we needed to watch Tony closely, there appeared to be no serious problem. The kidney was functioning properly, and the infections could be controlled with medication. I still felt very helpless and afraid. I couldn't talk to Chet because the look in his eyes revealed that he was feeling the same way.

Several months after this incident with Tony, I invited Christ into my life, and He began to work in me. One of the biggest things that happened right away was that great fear and worry I had been feeling concerning Tony left me. I heard a song that had a line in it that went something like "by His blood, I have no fear in me, I am set free." Those words played over and over in my mind, and I began to see that fear and worry are not from God, but are powerful tools of Satan. The Scriptures confirmed this.

> "I am leaving you with a gift. Peace of mind and heart! And the peace I give isn't fragile like the peace the world gives. So don't be troubled or afraid." John 14:27

"Don't be anxious about tomorrow; God will take care of your tomorrow too." Matthew 6:34

"For God hath not give us the spirit of fear, but of power and of love, and of a sound mind." II Timothy 1:7

"I sought the Lord and He heard me, and delivered my from all of my fears." Psalm 34:4

On and one the Scriptures went. I confessed this fear and worry to the Lord, and I stood on His Word, claiming what He had revealed to me. The spirit of fear was lifted, and I began to feel God's hand on us. I knew that Tony was apprehensive about all of his clinic appointments too, so I began to tell him about God's love. Every time we had a chance we would talk about Jesus. I would take every opportunity to tell Tony Bible stories, and soon he started to ask me for more. One day, when we were out riding, Tony invited Jesus into his life. He was a grown-up age five by this time, and he related that he had made a "very important decision." Our youngest son, David, was always with me too, and he heard all of the Bible stories I shared with Tony, but he was only two and did not appear ready to make a commitment. I prayed that one day he too would invite Jesus into his heart. After these things took place, I never again held that terrible fear. I felt cemented in God's care and felt I could trust Him for anything.

Shortly before Tony's seventh birthday, I made arrangements for his preschool check-up. The doctor had told us earlier that Tony had a heart murmur but assured us that a lot of kids have a heart murmur at one time or another when they are growing. This time, however, he felt because Tony also had the pelvic kidney it would be wise to do a more complete physical and check his heart too. When the doctor called with the results we were pretty stunned. He said that the x-rays revealed that Tony had a hole in his heart. The doctor wanted to make arrangements for us to see a specialist right away.

We had already learned that we were going to be moving, and were glad to discover that a pediatric cardiologist from a prominent metro hospital would be coming to Brainerd the first week we were to be there.

Our doctor also made all of the arrangements for Tony at a hearing clinic because it was discovered during further tests that Tony had a degree of deafness in his right ear, and had only one range of sound in his left ear. The ears themselves were fine, but the damage was in the nerve endings. This was all quite a bit to handle at one time, but the Lord took away any anxiety and gave me peace. I prayed that Chet and Tony would also sense God's presence and experience His peace. I had a strong feeling that the Lord was taking me through different steps where Tony was concerned, as if He were laying the groundwork to prepare us for a future time. This came clear to me following Tony's ear exam.

When Tony went for the hearing test, it was just a routine exam. We never dreamed that anything could be wrong. I sat in the small waiting area while Tony was with the doctor, and a man who looked very familiar to me came in the room. I was trying to place him when he saw me. He recognized me, and told me his name. We had been in the same class in high school. As soon as he said his name, I remembered him; however, something was very different about him. He knew right away what I was thinking because he said, "I see you've noticed the change in me." I turned a little red and told him that I did see that something had changed, but I couldn't put my finger on it. He refreshed my memory. All through school he was shy and withdrawn, almost appearing "spacey" as though he didn't know what was going on. It was due to a partial deafness. He walked around all of those years missing out on so much because he couldn't hear. He told me that his parents had taken him to several doctors but there was no known procedure to help a person with his particular hearing problem. As a result, he spent most of his life in a semi-silent state.

Just one year prior to our meeting, he was sent by an employer to have a complete physical exam including a hearing check. The ear specialist who examined him very excitedly told him that there had been a recent technique developed that helped people with his type of disability. He had the necessary tests, then surgery, and his hearing was restored to near perfect. The day I saw him he had just completed his one-year check-up and was doing great. Then, as we said our goodbyes, he said a strange thing as he turned to leave. "Don't worry about anything, maybe today there are no solutions or cures, but in 15 or 20 years there will be. I know; it happened that way with me." I thought what he said was peculiar, but when the doctor came out with the results of Tony's test, I found his words a comfort and I knew the Lord had placed that man there that day just for me.

There was no cure for the hearing problem that Tony had. The doctor told me that the nerve endings were dead in several places and there was no surgery or treatment that could change that. Instead of being upset, I left the clinic with a sense of hope because Jesus had assured me that I had no need to fear what might happen where Tony's hearing was concerned.

The Lord was preparing for the examination with the heart specialist, too. For several days before the appointment I began to get reassurances from the Scriptures like "A new heart also I will give you." (Ezekiel 36:26) and "He has sent Me to heal the brokenhearted."

The night before the appointment, just after I had prayed, I opened my copy of *Come Away My Beloved* and read these words: "Oh, My child, lay your heart in My hand, and let Me heal it." Then I turned the page and read, "Make it as tangible a transaction as possible, and visualize your own hand laying the physical organ of your heart in My hands; say to Me, Take this, Loving Master and wonderful Lord, and do with it as pleases Thee." [13] I closed my eyes and visualized the Lord standing there. As I approached Him with Tony, I saw Him reach into Tony's hands and take the heart Tony was holding out to Him. Tears came to my eyes and I felt myself being flooded with a peace beyond description. When I opened my eyes, I looked down at the Bible still opened on my lap and read a Scripture I hadn't noticed earlier. "He healeth the broken in heart and bindeth up their wounds." (Psalm 147:3)

The next day, as Tony and I were on our way to see the doctor, I told him what had happened, and he asked if he could close his eyes and imagine giving his heart to Jesus. We prayed, and Tony did as I had done the night before. When we conferred with the specialist about Tony and his x-rays, he told us that there was no indication of a hole in Tony's heart, and that he was disturbed that our pediatrician had alarmed us. He confirmed that there was a murmur, but it was nothing to be concerned about. Of course, we were glad to get the doctor's positive report, yet, I had a very strong feeling of "unfinished business." I thought of the first Scripture the Lord had given me: "A new heart will I give you," and I knew deep inside that the Lord would be doing more. Perhaps it was simply healing the heart murmur, or a reference to a spiritual healing. Whatever, I had peace and was confident that God was with us. I praised Him for all that had transpired and left future events in His hands.

Tony's health stayed pretty stable for about a year and a half after we had moved to Brainerd, then one afternoon, the school called and asked if we could come and get him. He had been complaining about a cramping in his side, and was doubled over with pain. The pain and cramping continued and our doctor began to be concerned that it could be kidney-related. He arranged an appointment with a pediatric urologist at the Mayo Clinic in Rochester.

At Mayo, both the urology and cardiology department did extensive tests. They told us that there was a heart murmur and a valve that wasn't opening and closing properly, but it didn't warrant any specific treatment. They also confirmed that Tony did have only one kidney, very flat and pancake-like in shape with one end folded over, and resting on the pelvic bone. It was functioning just fine; however, there was a small complication that would need immediate attention. We would be returning to Mayo in two weeks for surgery to correct the problem.

A few days before we were to go to Rochester for the surgery, I was busy ironing. Suddenly a heavy feeling came over me. It went through my body and felt like lead. All at once, I saw a clear picture in my mind. I saw an altar, and on the altar was a coffin. I was standing in front of it and was speaking to a church full of family and friends. I had a deep feeling of sadness, yet at the same time I felt a sense of joy. I was telling people about Tony, how his life had touched us, and how reassuring it was to know that he was with Jesus. Suddenly, the coffin was gone and so were all of the people. Only one person remained, a woman who attended my prayer group. The Lord told me to go to her and allow her to minister to me. I stepped down from the altar and walked over to her. She put her arms around me, and without ether of us uttering a single word, I felt a tremendous understanding come from her and move over me. (I did not know this at the time, but when I shared this experience with another friend, I learned that this woman had recently lost a son.) As she embraced me, I began to sob. The sobs were deep and very real. I was no longer seeing as in a vision, but I was in front of the ironing board alone. I could still feel arms around me, holding gently as I continued to sob. Waves of grief passed over me again and again. The grief came from a depth within me that I had no knowledge of possessing and it shook my body so I had to hold fast to the ironing board to keep from collapsing onto the floor. The feeling of grief suddenly lifted; the sobbing ceased. I knelt down and began to feel tears falling as I told the Lord that I would never choose that anything happen to Tony, but I knew that for all of us there would be peace only in God's will, and His will is what I wanted even if what I had seen in my vision would come to pass—Tony was the Lord's. The tears and the lead feeling disappeared and I felt a flood of love come over me. It would not stop but just continued. The contrast between what I had just experienced and the peace and perfect happiness I was now feeling was tremendous. I finished my ironing with a light and lifted feeling that continued throughout the day.

The following morning, the Lord led me to Genesis 22 when God tested the faith and obedience of Abraham. He asked Abraham to sacrifice his beloved son, Isaac. Abraham was obedient to God, and at the last minute, God spared the child, and provided a ram as an offering instead. I thought of the events I had just experienced and felt the Lord telling me that in my vision, I was asked to give up Tony, and even though I felt the deepest grief, sorrow, and pain, I wanted only to follow God's will. I knew that I had relinquished Tony into God's hands for all time and I knew that all would go well with his surgery and anything else that he would have to go through. Tony had his surgery and he came through it beautifully. He had the summer to recuperate, and was all healed, ready for school in the fall.

I remember that trip to Rochester—Chet and I decided that I should go alone with Tony and he would stay with David. As I was coming down the freeway, I was talking out loud to the Lord, commenting on the madness of freeway driving. I remember saying, "What is the purpose of my being on this highway? This freeway driving is way out of my league." Yet on the return trip, I was feeling very confident and decided I could handle it after all. I didn't know it at the time, but that drive was sort of an initiation into the big-city driving. It was only a short time later when driving the freeway was commonplace. I was grateful that the Lord had provided the chance to drive it alone when Tony and I went to Rochester. It was one less thing I had to concern myself about and it gave me the confidence to "hit the road" whenever I wanted to go anywhere.

After we had been in Shakopee for a number of months, I found a terrific doctor for myself, and I decided that she would be a good doctor for Tony too. It was time for him to have a checkup to see how well he had healed from the surgery he had when we lived in Brainerd, so I made an appointment. The doctor ordered x-rays and several other tests—kidney, bladder, heart, etc. I was glad that she was being so thorough. When she called me with the results, she reported that Tony had completely healed from his surgery and things looked good; in fact, she was pleased with all of his tests except one. "I just don't understand why you have never had that hole in Tony's heart repaired—it needs to be taken care of." I told her everything that we had been through with our pediatrician, the cardiac specialist, and the tests and x-rays at Mayo Clinic. Only our pediatrician thought there was a hole in his heart—no one else agreed with his findings.

"Well," she responded, "I believe he was right, and I think you should take Tony right back to Rochester and check this out." She said that she would make all of the arrangements and set up an appointment during the upcoming school vacation.

Tony woke up at five o'clock one morning complaining of a crushing feeling on his chest. He was experiencing difficulty breathing and was almost choking. Chet rushed him to the hospital and I stayed with David until I could make arrangements for a neighbor to come over. While I waited for her, I prayed. I also read the devotion in *God Calling* for that day (May 15). It said, "What can I say to you. Your heart is torn. Then remember He bindeth up the broken hearts—just feel the tenderness of My hands as I bind up the wounds."

When Tony woke up with the symptoms in his chest, Chet and I thought that he was having a heart attack I was confident that God had everything under control. By the time I drove to the hospital, the day was bright and beautiful and I couldn't help thinking what a beautiful day to go home to the Lord. I was in awe that I could even have a thought like that and still have such deep peace and calm, but that is how the Lord worked in me. When I got to the hospital I saw the relief in Chet's eyes—it wasn't Tony's heart, but an infection instead. The incident caused the doctor to suggest we go to Mayo Clinic right away, and within a few days we had an appointment.

Tony's tests were something else! The pediatric cardiologist couldn't find a thing. They showed me their x-rays and the x-rays that my doctor had sent, and they didn't look at all the same. Our doctor had sent a letter along with the x-rays she had done and urged them to be as thorough as possible because she was the second doctor to suspect a hole in the heart. They made it clear that finding a hole would be extremely remote, but they scheduled an appointment to do a heart catherization to satisfy her and to convince us once and for all that everything was fine.

The following Sunday morning, I was getting ready to go to church. Tony and I would be leaving for Rochester in the afternoon. His heart cath was to be done on Monday, and he had to be in the hospital by Sunday evening. Before I left for church, I asked the Lord if He would give me an indication of what was ahead. I picked up the Bible that was on the table in the hallway, opened it, and found myself reading Jeremiah 18:1-6. It was the Scripture about the potter and the clay, and how the jar the potter was working on wasn't right, so the potter kneaded it into a lump and started again. I thought over the verses on the way to church. I brought a small King James Bible to church with me that morning, and during the first hymn, I opened it up without looking at it and placed it on my lap. After the song, I looked down and saw that I had opened to Jeremiah 18:2—"And the vessel he made out of clay was marred at the hand of the potter. So he made it again another vessel, as seemed good to the potter to make it." I was so excited by this time that I started to share what had happened with a good friend who was sitting next to me. "What Scripture did you say it was?" she asked, but before I could answer, I heard the pastor's voice from the pulpit. "Jeremiah 18:2 is our text for today." He then proceeded to read the verse.

I was absolutely convinced that Tony had a hole in his heart. When I came home from church, I told Chet and Tony what I believed. I also told them that God was going to take care of everything. Chet told me to wait until the doctors made their decision, but I knew what the decision would be and all I planned to do was watch how God was going to work.

That evening, I stayed with Tony at the hospital until he began to fall asleep, then I went to the Holiday Inn. I decided to have something to eat before going to my room, but when I went into the dining room, I immediately felt uncomfortable. Everyone was there with someone, and I was very much alone. The waitress seated me and as I looked over the menu, I grew even more uncomfortable. At every table there was talking and laughter. I couldn't remember if I had ever eaten alone in a restaurant before. I placed my order, then I rummaged through my purse for a small booklet I had shoved in there a while ago. Just as I pulled it out, the waitress brought my salad. "Lord," I whispered, "It is going to feel so funny eating alone. Please lift this alone feeling from me and help me to remember that You are with me. Sit by me and be my companion." I picked up the booklet I had set on the table. It was called, "My Heart Christ's Home" by R.B. Munger. I opened it and read, "He seated Himself at the table with me and asked, 'What's on the menu for dinner?'" [14] I almost shouted out loud. I ate the meal and it was wonderful. I didn't feel alone anymore—how could I? I was in the company of the King of Kings. He made His presence known to me and made it a dinner I would never forget. I ate many meals with the Lord in the days to come, and never felt conspicuous or self-conscious again.

That night I slept soundly. I had great peace knowing that in the morning the doctors would find a hole in Tony's heart and God would be in the details. The next day after the tests were completed, I met with several doctors. They confirmed what the Lord had told me. Tony had a hole between the top chamber of his heart, an atrium-ceptal defect. They scheduled Tony for surgery in two weeks.

Tony and I had already talked about all of this and he appeared to be prepared to have the surgery. On the ride home from Rochester he said, "I'll be okay, Mom. I'm not scared at all." I felt prepared too. The Lord had spoken to me so many times about this that I felt very calm. The Scripture in Jeremiah reassured me that God was indeed going to repair Tony's heart. I knew that He had chosen to work through the doctors at Mayo Clinic.

What I wasn't prepared for was the reaction from other people in my family. I could sense their worry and concern but I couldn't seem to convince them that God was going to take care of everything. When I appeared not to worry, they became upset with me. My mother especially had a hard time with my attitude. "You are so cold and unfeeling—don't you even care?" she asked me one day. Care? I cared more than anyone could know and I was concerned. I loved Tony and David and Chet with all my heart and the thought of any of them having to go through this kind of ordeal was very painful to me. There were many tears, but only the Lord saw them, and He dried them. There were questions, and He answered them. I hurt for Tony, and I would never have chosen this path for him, but I knew that God loved him far more than I ever could, and if this was His divine plan, I could accept it knowing He would work it out. He had prepared me and I knew I could trust Him completely. I could not deny the trust and peace I felt; it was real.

I knew the agony Chet was going through, too. His sadness and grief over the whole situation was very strong; you just had to look at him to see it in his eyes. He carried most of it himself and had difficulty talking about his feelings. I really wanted to share my peace with him, but I knew that he had to deal with this in his own way. I couldn't force my attitude on him. I prayed that God would hold him up and give him comfort where I couldn't. I prayed that God would use whatever it took to draw Chet into a closer walk with Him and I knew that He could use all of this to do that.

David had a special way to handle all of the things concerning Tony. On their daily drives to Rochester, Chet would explain all about

Tony's surgery, doctors, hospitals and hearts. On one of these trips, Dave had heard enough explanations and decided to change the subject. "Okay, Dad, let's just talk turtles," and they had a big discussion without mentioning Tony. Dave also needed to "talk to God" a lot during this time. We lived less than a block away from our church, and on several occasions he would announce, "I gotta go talk to God now," and up the street he would go. When his talk was over, he would come back home and resume his activities.

It was July 16, 1980, the day of Tony's surgery. My Pastor and his wife made the trip to Rochester to spend the day with me. Their prayers, concern, and friendship were a blessing and so uplifting. It was a tremendous comfort for me to have them there. In addition to praying with me, they ministered to several others who were in the waiting lounge. While Tony was still in surgery, they left to visit another patient they knew.

Once during my time of waiting, while Tony was undergoing surgery, a wave of despair passed over me. I had been sitting very still when suddenly I felt something move into the lounge. It passed over me like a slight breeze, only it wasn't gentle, and it settled on me like a blanket. Suddenly, I had knots in my stomach and my heart was pounding hard. What if something went wrong in surgery? What if the doctors couldn't do anything? What if Tony was going to die? In just a few seconds, panic and fear filled my body. I wanted to cry out. I got up and went into the restroom. It was empty, so I spoke out loud to the Lord, praying something like this: "Jesus, I have had such a calm and peace, and now it has been taken away and I have all this fear and anxiety. I know it's not from You, and I know that no matter what, You are in control. You are keeping Tony, and You will keep me, too. I trust You with Tony's life. I take authority over this fear and rebuke it in Jesus' name—there is no place in me for it. I'm going to keep on trusting You, Lord, and I praise and thank You." As suddenly as the heavy feeling had settled on me, it left as soon as I prayed. I could actually feel it "lift off of me" and leave the room. My peace had returned and I felt calm again.

When I returned to the lounge, I noticed a Bible on a corner table. I opened it and put my finger down on the words, "Don't be frightened,

Mary." (Luke 1:30) My heart felt so warm within me. This was so personal, and there are no words to describe what Jesus did for me in that moment, but His presence was so real and powerful that I felt I could reach out and actually touch Him.

It took several hours to complete the surgery and then another hour or more in recovery, but soon, my name was called. Tony would be coming up to the intensive care unit and I would be able to see him for a few minutes. Pastor and his wife had returned and we prayed together. I asked the Lord for a Scripture and read Hosea 6:12: "Come, let us return to the Lord; it is He who has torn us and He will heal us. He has wounded, He will bind us up. In just a couple of days, or three at the most, He will set us on our feet again to live in His kindness." This was a very familiar passage to me. It had been a blessing in the past and I felt that the Lord used it again to assure me that all was well.

When I walked into the intensive care unit I was greeted by a nurse. I asked her how long Tony would be in intensive care. Imagine my delight when she replied, "Oh, a couple of days, or three at the most, then he'll soon be on his feet again." When I came to the bed Tony was in, all I saw was his face at first. It looked so soft and seemed to be surrounded by a mist. I was told beforehand that all patients had a trach tube that would remain in for several days after surgery, but Tony had none. He smiled as soon as I said his name. Pastor had come into the room and prayed with us before he had to leave. When he left, I stood looking at Tony's face, silently praising God that Tony's hand was in mine and that he had come through the surgery just fine. As I looked at Tony, the mist that had surrounded his face began to subside, and as it did, I began to see the incision and all of the tubes in him and the equipment around him, and I realized that the Lord had worked another miracle so that I would gently be made aware of everything. This was even more of a blessing when I saw the reactions of others upon first seeing a loved one in this state.

Another miracle was the trach tube. It was the one thing that Tony had been apprehensive about. There were a number of children that had a similar surgery during the time we were there, and Tony was the only one who came from recovery without it. Another praise for the Lord! There was one more thing that I considered a miracle: in all the time Tony went through everything, he never once uttered a single word of complaint. Never once a "why me," no moans, no groans, no negative reactions. His attitude from the beginning was one of total acceptance. Once out of intensive care, he had many questions about the tubes, the equipment, etc., but his attitude remained wonderful.

God had brought us through and I knew that He would never fail us. It had been easy to trust Him for Tony's surgery. He had prepared me for it and proved over and over again that He would take care of everything.

"He will keep in perfect peace all those who trust in Him,
whose thoughts turn often to the Lord." Isaiah 26:3

Whatever It Takes

When I first began my walk with the Lord, I made it a practice to pray every evening, but after we moved to the cities, my evenings became busier and it was difficult to make time at night. I began to pray in the morning instead, and as I visited with the Lord, I found myself wanting a deeper, closer relationship with Him. I was enjoying the Lord for myself and I treasured my time alone with Him. It was as though I was trying to contain Him in my own little space, shutting myself away with Him to the exclusion of the rest of the world. But then my prayer time would end and I would move on with my day, going out into the world, many times leaving the Lord until morning came again.

The Lord wanted me to see Him all present at all times, in all circumstances, and to be free to worship Him at all times. He wanted me to see His presence not only during my quiet time, but constantly. I needed to be more trusting, more sure of Him, and more open to His leading in my life. I had to live the truth in His Word—that He is with me ALWAYS, not only at my chosen time. I began to pray that He would work this out in my heart and life.

One Sunday morning during church service, I realized that I had been putting a lot of things before the Lord. I prayed that He would remove anything in my life that was in the way of my total surrender to Him and to all He had planned for me. As these thoughts were going through my mind, a guest vocalist began to sing a song called "Whatever It Takes." [15] I didn't recall the entire song, but the words to the chorus made such an impression on me that I wrote some of them down, as closely a I could remember, and this became my daily prayer over the next months.

> "Whatever it takes to draw closer to You,
> That's what I'm willing to do.
> Whatever it takes for my will to break,
> That's what I'm willing to do.
> If through sorrow and pain more like You I'll become,
> That's what I'm willing to do.
> Take the dearest things from me if that's what it takes
> For a closer walk, Lord, with You."

I had such a peace praying those words, and I believed they truly were the desire of my heart. I had already turned Chet and the boys over to the Lord, and I knew that He loved them far more than I ever could. I also knew that all I had—all my possessions—were His to take anytime. I wanted Jesus more than anyone or anything and I was not afraid to say that prayer. I believed that God knew what was best for me and what it would take for a closer, more committed and intimate walk with Him. Even when Tony faced surgery, I could still pray that prayer, even the part about "taking the dearest things from me."

Yet, deep in my heart was a feeling that something was in the way—something the Lord wanted from me. I couldn't understand what it could be, but I knew that it would be revealed to me in God's good time.

When we first discovered that Tony needed to go to Rochester, we used our savings to finance the trip and the lodging, food, etc., and we weren't thinking very conservatively. Costs kept adding up, but we were so involved in Tony's health that we were oblivious to the mounting debt. Even when we found out there would be more extensive tests, financial matters never entered the picture. We had insurance through Chet's company and a little savings account. When heart surgery was the next step, our main focus was Tony. He needed the surgery right away, and that was that. I knew that God was handling things, and I believed everything would just fall into place.

Now, as I look back, I am amazed at how quickly that happy trust in the Lord's provision that had been so present during Tony's ordeal changed into uneasiness and concern. Suddenly every time I turned around I was withdrawing money from our savings. The bills from the first tests had come in. The amount the insurance company covered turned out to be only for certain specific things, leaving us with a higher amount to pay back than we had anticipated. We thought that we would be able to make most of the payments, when troubles with the car surprised us and several other unexpected household expenses developed. In addition to that, the raise Chet had been promised for almost two years didn't materialize. I called the hospital to arrange payments, only to discover that they demanded full payment on everything—and we hadn't even received the statement for the heart surgery yet! When that finally arrived, the cost almost blew us away. I was still praising God for Tony's recovery and for all He had brought us through, but I was very anxious about the bills. Hmmm—trust in the Lord? Appears that I temporarily forgot about that—I was praying like mad, but the trust factor had diminished considerably as my prayers became more of the hand-wringing type filled with ideas of what I thought the Lord should do.

Chet and I sat down one evening and tried to get things into perspective. Chet was particularly upset. Our move to Shakopee had been a financial bummer. In addition to bills from our previous house that we were still paying, the house itself had been on the market for a year and a half before it sold at a loss. There were so many new commitments on our present house, plus the broken promises from the company and a cutback in wages. We were just beginning to see a little progress when we came face to face with all of this new responsibility. We decided that with the help of new loans we could handle the balance of medical bills. We also made the decision that I would go back to work. Even though I was a little apprehensive because I hadn't worked for 10 years, I went ahead and called the school business office to sign up for substitute teaching.

The day after the big decision to return to work, I was involved with cleaning, doing laundry, and preparing food for company. I had promised my neighbor that I would watch her two boys, and they were busy in the family room playing with Tony and Dave. I had just leaned over to put some of my folded laundry into a bottom drawer when I began to see funny lights in my eyes as if I had looked into the flash of a camera. I could partially see, but the little flashes of light continued. They danced around everything I looked at and I thought that I must have moved suddenly or stood up too quickly. It took about half an hour, but they finally diminished enough for me to start working on a dessert I had planned for my company.

I turned to put the dessert into the refrigerator when Dave came into the kitchen to ask me a question. I was still leaning over into the fridge when I answered him. I remember thinking how far away and echo-sounding my voice was. He kept repeating the question and I kept answering. I turned toward Dave and saw the most frightened look on his face. "Mom, what's wrong, are you okay?" I opened my mouth to speak, but only gibberish came out. My voice sounded far, far away in the back of my head, and even though my thoughts were clear, my speech was not. By this time the other kids had come into the kitchen all looking terrified. I tried to tell them not to worry, but my talking only made them more upset. I took out a paper and wrote, "Tony, call dad. Tell him to come home because I don't feel well." I handed the note to Tony, only he couldn't read it—it was only filled with lines and chicken scratchings. I tried to write the phone number, but I couldn't remember it. Fortunately, Tony knew what to do and he immediately called Chet and told him to hurry home.

I went into the bedroom to lie down. I didn't know what was going on, and except for being a little puzzled about all that I had experienced over the course of an hour, I felt just fine. I closed my eyes and touched my finger to my nose. I could do that without any problem. Then, I touched each finger with my thumb—no problem there either. I tried to pray, but I could not speak clearly. I began to pray in tongues—perfect! There is no trouble when it's the Holy Spirit doing the work. I was very calm and quite surprised that I was not feeling frightened or nervous. I was fully aware that I had lost a portion of my vision, my ability to speak, and my motor skills, yet I had a strong sense that the Lord was by my side. I continued to pray in the Spirit—it was the only thing I could do.

When I got up and returned to the living room, Tony brought me a newspaper and asked if I could read it to him. He told me to follow his finger and read very slowly. I was able to say each little word as he pointed to it. The bigger words were still pretty garbled and when I tried a sentence, it was even more difficult. We kept at it and by the time Chet came home I was able to say a few words very slowly.

Chet was positive that I'd had a stroke. I tried to tell him that I didn't think so, but when he heard me mumbling, he almost fainted. He called the clinic, piled all the kids in the car and took me to see the doctor. The doctor asked me several questions; by then, it was getting easier to answer and my speech slowly began to return to normal. My vision was still acting like I was looking through a kaleidoscope, and when he asked me to look at a calendar that was on the wall in front of me, I could only see half of it. For example, when I looked at the word August, I could only see "gust"; as I moved my head in different directions, I could only see portions of anything I looked at. The doctor told me that he would be putting me into the hospital where they would do a more extensive assessment.

Before Chet brought me to the hospital, we stopped at home to pick up a few things and to arrange for a neighbor to take the kids. I grabbed my Bible and a few devotional books and took them with me. By the time I was settled into the hospital bed, my speech and vision had almost cleared up to a normal state. I asked the Lord to shed some light on why I was there. I opened one of the books that I brought with me and read, "You do not realize that you would have broken down under the weight of your cares but for this renewing time with Me. All your movements, your goings and comings, controlled by Me. Not only now in the hour of your difficulty, but from this time forth and forevermore." I opened another book and read, "You are not a stray and uncared for. You belong to the Secret Service of Heaven. There are privileges and protections for you along the way." I knew that Jesus was with me and that He had permitted all of these things.

I closed my eyes and thanked the Lord for giving me peace and the assurance of His presence. I reflected over the events I had just been through—the loss of speech, vision, and motor skills—and as I thought these things, I heard a voice say, "And what "of these things" Mary? Are you willing also that I take these dearest things from you if it were the only way?"

It would be a while before I had the chance to reflect on what the Lord had said to me, for at just that moment, the doctor came into the room. He told me that he was sending me to Mayo Clinic for neurological tests in the hope that they would be able to shed some light on what was wrong. I spent several days in Rochester seeing and talking to a number of doctors. I felt fine, but so exhausted and drained that all I wanted to do was rest. I was blessed to have a Christian nurse and being able to talk to her about the Lord was so uplifting and refreshing. I had an elderly woman as my roommate and I was able to share my testimony with her. Clearly, there were several reasons God had permitted this episode in my life. There was still some unfinished business, but the Lord had not yet made it plain to me.

The doctors said that I did not have a stroke, but rather something called a migraine phenomena. It is common in people who have had severe headaches for years. The phenomena generally takes place before the onset of a migraine headache, or following one. I have had less than five headaches in my entire life—one occurred when I was in the third or fourth grade that had me crying from the pain, another when a board fell on my head, and one that lasted two days when I stopped drinking coffee with caffeine. I shared that with the doctors and they said that in my case it could have been due to something I ate (or didn't eat), a fast movement, excitement, or extreme exertion (that one isn't very likely—my most strenuous exercise is inhaling and exhaling which I do around the clock and have every intention to keep doing). They also told me that there was no way to know if this was a one-time event, or if it would begin to happen frequently. After I came back home, I began to get back to a regular routine. School had started and I decided to keep my name on the sub list. I really didn't want to, but I prayed and felt led to be submissive and do as Chet wished. I trusted that the Lord would open the doors if this was His will for me, or close them if it wasn't. I was back on schedule with my prayer time, too, and my main prayer was for the Lord to show me what all the things I had been through meant, especially where my relationship with Him was concerned.

One morning, as I was praying, I thought of the prayer that I had prayed so faithfully, "Whatever it takes..." I realized that I had not said it once since I was in the hospital and I remembered the words the Lord spoke to me "What of these things?" Now it became clear. I had prayed "take the dearest things from me" never dreaming that the "these things" would be so very much a part of me—my speech, my vision, my motor skills. I looked at my husband, sons, other relationships, possessions, etc., and deemed them "most dear", but the Lord was opening my eyes and giving me a new perspective as to what the dearest things really were. Would I be able to give them up for Him?

In addition to revealing this to me, the Lord was also helping me to see how much faith I had been putting in our savings account, Chet's wages, and our insurance company. My concern over medical bills had me pacing the floor, and my attitude ranged from anger to frustration. It only increased when my short stay in the hospital added thousands of dollars to our existing debt. I thought that subbing would help to get us through, but I hadn't even had a chance at that yet.

Worry, fear, anger, doubt, and blame against everyone from the insurance company to the people demanding payments—the Lord impressed upon me that I should write down the areas that I had relied on, the things I had chosen to do rather than trust Him. I made two columns—in one I felt led to list the things I had done and in the other column to write the things I was going to do to correct each of them. As I wrote my list in the first column, I began to feel tears welling up in my eyes. It was a pretty impossible task I was about to undertake—to undo the mess I had made of things was going to take a lot more than I had in me. It was hopeless. I didn't even know what to do with the first thing I had written down, and I had a whole list to go through. How could all of this have cropped up? I was sobbing by now, repenting of my sin and confessing before the Lord—I knew that I couldn't go on. I had to calm down and get back to this another time.

Reading always had a calming affect on me, so I looked through a stack of books. My eyes fell on one that was new, and I remembered finding it at the book store—it was the cheapest one on the half-price rack. I had never gotten around to reading it, so I decided now would be a good time. I looked at the title, *Lessons from the Furnace.*

Great, I thought, *this should be a real uplifting read!* As I walked to the chair, I opened the book and stopped dead in my tracks as I read, "I want you to write down every sin that has been bugging you." I had just done that, and suddenly I couldn't wait to read more. The next thing I read was, "Then, go before God this day and officially forgive yourself sin by sin as you know Jesus has already forgiven you." [16] Hallelujah! Praise God! Talk about eyes being opened. Jesus had been faithful and had forgiven me the moment I repented of my sin. I picked up the sheet I had written the two columns on and wrote the words, "What would God do?" Then I wrote the verse from I John 1:9, "If we confess our sins, He is faithful and just to forgive us and cleanse us from all unrighteousness." Then, I read each of the sins I had listed and forgave myself just as Jesus had forgiven me. As I did , I crossed out each one so I couldn't read it anymore, and just let it be gone forever.

I felt so good after all of this, and decided to read a portion of a devotional I had. I opened to a page and began reading, "Be of good cheer. Sing and be glad, for this day is a day of victory and a day of deliverance. This day is a day of joy, yes, to My own heart, for I delight to answer prayer and to make the crooked straight. I will restore and bless a hundredfold."

By this time, I was in such a wonderful mood, I couldn't stop thanking God. He proceeded to reveal verses to me in the Bible that were like a recap of all that I had experienced. He began by leading me to a passage in Isaiah 30:1-2:

> "Woe to my rebellious children, says the Lord, for without consulting me, You have gone down to Egypt to find aid and have put your trust in Pharaoh for his protection."

Following that, a verse in Jeremiah 4:1-2 said,

> "O, Israel, [I substituted my name to read "Oh, Mary Ann"] if you will truly turn to Me and absolutely discard your idols and if you will swear by Me alone the Living God...My name will be glorified."

Then I read Isaiah 30:18, 20-22—

> "Yet the Lord still waits for you to come to Him, so He can show you His love; He will conquer you to bless you, just as He said for the Lord is faithful to His promises. Blessed are all those who wait for Him to help them. Though He give you the bread of adversity and water of affliction, yet He will be with you to teach you and with your own eyes you will see your teacher. And if you leave God's paths and go astray, you will hear a voice behind you say, no, this is the way; walk here, and you will destroy all your silver idols and golden images and cast them out."

The verses helped me to see that I had put my trust in all kinds of things: savings accounts, requests to relatives who turned us down, banks, a loan from Chet's company, advice from everyone and anyone, etc. Even the subbing was a grab at something other than the Lord. I realized that God could use every one of these avenues to work in our behalf, but I had put my trust in them rather than in Jesus, our real source.

Isaiah 30:1-2 revealed what I had done—I had been rebellious, seeking help from everyone but the Lord. Jeremiah 4:1-2 impressed upon me that I was to set aside my idols (things I just mentioned). That's what I did when I wrote my list, and confessed my sin. Isaiah 30:18-22 showed me that the Lord would patiently wait for me to come back to Him. The verses that the Lord led me to after I had reached this point were in Jonah chapter 2. "I had lost all hope and turned my thoughts once more to the Lord", and "Because I have returned to Him, He is able to deliver me!" I felt as if the big, ugly fish of despair had spit me up onto the warm, sunny beach of God's love and provision.

Over the next few days, I read the entire book *Lessons from the Furnace* by Bob Heil, and God continued to minister to me, teaching me how to remain cool in the "fiery furnace," to look not so much for an escape from our problems, but to look for God in each situation.

God began to demonstrate to me what His miracle provision is like, and He used many lessons that helped to sustain me through the furnace. In the next pages, I am going to share a few of them, not with any particular time element, because when they took place was not as important as that they happened, and through each one, God taught me something. Some were painful, some joyful; some took minutes, others took days; but all of them gave me a clearer insight into myself and a stronger, deeper love for the Lord.

Sitting on the Butter

I have already shared the attitudes and lack of trust I displayed when we were experiencing financial difficulties, and how the Lord dealt with me and led me through all of those trials on to victory. He proved faithful in all of our circumstances and He met all of our needs.

It was during the time when our focus was on bills, bills, bills. They arrived daily and ate up all of our savings, including the small amount of money we'd set aside in the boys' accounts. In addition, the company Chet worked for announced a wage freeze. I wrote to creditors explaining our situation and found many of them helpful. In most instances, our payments were cut in half, helping us with our credit card debt. The medical bills, however, were another story.

Medical bills do not come in one big lump. They come from everywhere—clinics, doctors' offices, hospitals, surgeons, anesthesiologists, medical tests and supplies, follow-up appointments, and on and on. Some of them were reasonable, and we paid them with money from our savings. One of the clinic bills was large and insurance coverage paid only a portion of it, leaving us with a balance of $7500. We had already used money from a bank loan to pay the most demanding debt, and our savings were gone, but I was confident that the Lord was going to take care of everything.

The days turned into weeks and there was no money to make the payment. In fact, the portion the insurance company was to pay hadn't come through either. I continued to pray, but one afternoon, I asked the Lord what I was doing wrong. Hadn't I been trusting Him? Hadn't I told everyone that He'd handle it? Hadn't I expected a miracle? I felt the Lord tell me that He knew I was trusting Him and I just needed to continue to trust even if it was difficult, even if I didn't see an answer come. As I was talking to God, the phone rang. It was Chet. "Wait until you hear this," he said, "the insurance company sent us a check for that one clinic."

"How much?" I asked.

"That's the part I can't wait to tell you. They decided to pay the entire amount!"

"What about the $7500 we owe?" I responded.

"That's included too," Chet answered, "They paid 100%!" Praise the Lord—I had a praise and thank you time all that afternoon.

I thought a lot about that day and the miracle with our finances, but I wondered how many times and with how many bills the Lord would do the same thing. One morning, after Chet left for work, I listened to a Christian radio program while I did my chores. I heard the neatest little story that erased any doubts about God's continued provision. The story was about two frogs who fell into a vat of cream. One was convinced they would never get out—nothing could be worse, he said, there's too much of it to drink, it's too deep to stand in, no one can hear our cries for help, so he gave up and he drowned. The other frog never gave up hope that he would be rescued. He kept his head above the cream and kept treading it as though it were water. He continued treading all through the night. In the morning he was near exhaustion, but croaking happily, safe and secure on the top of a mound of butter! I knew the story was another illustration of patience and I knew that God was using it to encourage me to stay the course and not lose heart.

I couldn't wait for Chet to come home, so I called him at work to tell him the story. "I know the Lord's telling us to hang in there, we're going to be like the frog that made it." Right after our conversation, I sat down to read from the Bible. I read Psalm 30 and was touched by the fifth verse, "Weeping may endure for a night, but joy cometh in the morning." It seemed to be one more assurance that all was going to be just fine.

That afternoon, my mom and my in-laws came for a visit and my mother-in-law handed me an envelope. I opened it up and couldn't believe my eyes. It contained $1000. I called Chet right away and said, "Praise the Lord! We're on the butter!" He knew right away what I meant.

There were so many more miracles ahead concerning our finances, and as the days passed we were able to see God moving us to victory not only where money issues were concerned, but in other areas too.

A Meeting of the Minds

After I became a Christian, I noticed that my view on many issues changed. Things that I had approved of before could no longer be part of my framework of thinking. I needed to stand on the Word of God and I could not get into a position of compromise. I knew that the Lord was revealing His truth to me, and I saw myself changing little by little.

I was most aware of these changes in my thinking when I was with a group of friends or family members. Often the discussions would revolve around religious, political, or social topics. These talks would always put me on one side of the fence, while everyone else stood on the other. My opinion usually inspired eye-rolling, head-shaking, and smirking results.

One afternoon, Chet and I were visiting with our family. I knew that at some point in the visit someone would bring up something that I did not support. I knew, too, that I would speak out and share my ideas. As I expected, the conversation turned to a controversial subject, one that I was totally in disagreement with, and one that had the support of everyone else there. As the discussion went on, I began to form the words in my mind that I would use to illustrate the Biblical viewpoint on the topic.

Finally, the conversation had escalated to a point where I could keep still no longer, and I opened my mouth to speak—when Chet began to talk. I was totally taken by surprise when he spoke practically word for word everything I had been ready to say. This was more than a coincidence; it was a miracle.

Now, at last, I understood. When we were still in Brainerd, I had been praying that Chet would come into a relationship with the Lord. During that time, the Lord assured me that He was working in Chet's life. He told me to look for "a meeting of the minds." I did not know what that was, and I had no further word from the Lord on the subject, but, in His good time, He made it all clear to me. In the years that followed, Chet and I have come into agreement on more and more of the same outlook and position on a wide range of issues. We truly have experienced the meeting of the minds the Lord spoke of.

Someone's Knocking at the Door

One Sunday evening at prayer meeting, we had a teaching on Revelation 3:20: "Behold, I stand at the door and knock. If any man hear My voice and open the door I will come in and sup with him and he with Me." The teaching went beyond the talk of an initial salvation experience; it included our daily walk with the Lord and the turning over of all phases of our lives to Him. We were asked to close our eyes and imagine opening up the door to Jesus. For some who were in attendance, I believe it was the first time they opened their hearts' doors to invite Christ to be their Savior and Lord. For others, it provided a chance to reflect on their commitment to the Lord. Others became aware of areas where Jesus had been barred from their lives, and where they needed to be more yielded and open.

I closed my eyes and imagined that I was in my kitchen when I heard a knock at the door. I opened it up to find Jesus standing there. I invited Him in, and after I pictured Him stepping into the room, my thoughts seemed to be turned off and I experienced a real vision of what was taking place. I could see Jesus and me in the kitchen as if I were an observer at a play. There was a meal prepared and I began to serve Him. There were candles on the table and beautiful china. I could see that I had the room all clean and I felt good that I had taken the time to prepare a special meal. I watched as we sat eating, talking and laughing. When the meal was finished, I began to gather up the dirty dishes. My back was to the Lord as I picked up the plates and glasses, and when I turned around, I was surprised to see the Lord standing at the sink. His sleeves were rolled up and He was tying on a white apron. He began to wash the dishes as I brought them to Him. We continued our conversation as we dried them and cleaned up together.

I was wonderfully impressed by all that I saw in this vision. Isn't it just like Jesus to use such a practical, down-to-earth experience like this to illustrate such great truths! When we open the door to Jesus, He doesn't just come in as a casual observer, He comes in and takes an active part in our lives. There is no area that is too small or insignificant, and He is concerned about them all. What a perfect example of service—

the King of Kings Himself donning an apron and performing the task of washing dishes. His desire is to be with us, share Himself with us, and be a part of everything we are involved in. I reflected on all of the times I had finished praying and went off to take care of a million things, forgetting all about the Lord. The whole experience had a profound effect on me. It gave me the assurance that I am never alone, to do the work alone, but Jesus is with me, and He is not just an observer in my life but an active participant working by my side.

I remembered how many guests I had entertained who made a quick exit when it was time to clean up. I remembered how many times I was a guest and, rather than roll up my sleeves and pitch in to help, I had left the work for someone else. I even recalled times that I did help, but it was under protest, or perhaps to impress. So often we want to leave tasks for others to do because we feel they are "beneath us" or we are too busy, or we just prefer to leave everything for later. But, when Jesus enters our lives He comes in to stay and work with us no matter what, until all is accomplished and completed within us. Philippians 1:6 says, "And I am certain that God who began the good work within you will keep right on helping you until His task within you is finally finished on that day when Christ returns."

Our Lord is truly faithful, and He is committed to us once we are His. He works in us, and by His very example, we learn of our responsibilities and commitment to one another.

The Rock and the Hard Place

The book of Acts describes the effect that the coming of the Holy Ghost had on believers. Their lives were dramatically changed. We know they were given the power to witness; they were given a "holy boldness" to share the gospel. They were also given the desire to be more of a community, sharing possessions and money and food, and gathering together for prayer and more in-depth fellowship and communion with each other. What an example for us in prayer groups and church families! Commitment isn't easy. It means giving unselfishly of your time and talent, often setting aside your own agenda to help others.

The prayer group that I attended had a strong commitment to one another. There were a number of ministries operating that kept the group alive and healthy. The leaders of the group, under the guidance of the Holy Spirit, made a written commitment to each other and to everyone in the group. I admired those in the leadership group and those who had taken on the work in the various ministries, but unlike Jesus in my vision, I did not want to roll up my sleeves and pitch in. It was much easier to let others do it. When I was approached and asked if I would participate in the pre-prayer ministry before each prayer meeting, I delayed giving them an answer. I told them that I wanted to pray about it before I made any commitment, but it was more than that.

Sunday night was always busy, and preparing supper and spending time with the boys and Chet already had me rushing around before I finally ran out the door for the prayer meeting. Agreeing to be in the pre-prayer ministry would mean that I would have to be serious about getting to meetings at least 45 minutes ahead of time. In addition, people would be depending on me, and I didn't know if I could handle one more responsibility. I didn't want to say no when I was asked, but I didn't want to commit either. I needed to seek Jesus for guidance and direction.

"What do you want me to do, Lord? I feel like I am between a rock and a hard place. If I say no, I will feel like I am letting them down. If I say yes, I will feel like I would be putting more pressure on myself." The Lord's answer was clear. "When you are between a rock and a hard place, you need to get on the rock, which is Christ, and He will give you victory over the hard place." I could see that the hard place in this situation was me. I could be stubborn, selfish, and focused on my needs, but when I put my trust in Jesus (the Rock) and allow Him to work things out in me, I have victory. There are several Scriptures that refer to Jesus as the Rock. Deuteronomy 32:4 says "He is the Rock! His Word is perfect." Psalm 62:2 tells us that "He alone is my Rock, my rescuer, defense, and fortress." And from Psalm 18:2: "He is my Savior, a rock where none can reach me, a tower of safety. For who is God except our Lord? Who but He is as a Rock!"

God led me to say "yes" to the commitment to join the pre-prayer ministry and I was blessed greatly by it. God, as usual, worked out all of the details, even moving Chet to assume the duty of "chief cook and cleaner-upper" every Sunday evening. I was able to get to every meeting on time and never felt any undue stress or pressure.

The Lord gave me a sense of being needed at the same time He used me to fill a need. He taught me that sincere commitment made with His guidance is a joy, not a burden. We don't have to be afraid to take on a new challenge or become more deeply involved. Trusting God to guide us is the key. If something is not for us, He will make it plain and close the doors. If it is His will for us, He will prepare the way and give us the strength and ability to do it. It is so much better to stand on the Rock than to struggle between the rock and the hard place. God also showed me that He is not only a rock to stand on, but to hide behind and rest within. He is our protector, our place of safety, "a place to go in time of trouble." No wonder we can trust Him.

The Dangers of the Day

Many times, I read a portion of Scripture over and over, and although I can have many thoughts on its meaning, it doesn't really come alive for me until I have a personal experience to go along with it. It is one thing to read that God is a rock, a place of safety, but it is another thing to really know it beyond a shadow of doubt.

One winter night I was driving home on a very dark road. The boys were with me and we all commented on the extent of the blackness. I normally went on the highway, but this evening we were all anxious to get home, so I took a shortcut on one of the back roads. There were no lights except for my car lights, which barely made a dent in the darkness. Because I was not very familiar with the road, having been on it only once before—and that had been in the daytime. I chose to drive very slowly. The drive seemed to be taking forever and I could see that taking the highway would have been a much wiser choice.

Suddenly, a large black shape moved in front of the car. It was so dark out I couldn't make out what it was. The form cut in front of us and bumped along my side of the car. Before the boys or I could say a word, another form moved in front of the car and did the same thing. I could hear very heavy breathing and realized that there were two large horses running on the road. They must have gotten loose from a nearby farm. None of us said a word for over a minute, then the boys started talking excitedly.

"Wow, that was cool! We didn't even panic or anything, Mom!" one of them said, and I realized that it was true. Through the entire episode, we were all so calm and the whole atmosphere in the car had been peaceful.

I reached the main road and turned onto the first driveway. I made my way up to the end of the driveway and discovered a young couple talking to two policemen who were still in their car. They were telling the officers that two of their horses had gotten out of the fence. I told them what had just happened. They were grateful that we weren't hurt and thanked us for stopping.

As soon as I got home, I went directly to my Bible. I said no word to the Lord, as a matter of fact, except for thinking "what's going on, Lord?" when I was in the car, I didn't pray at all. I simply opened the Bible and read, "Now you don't need to be afraid of the dark anymore, nor fear the dangers of the day; nor dread the plagues of darkness, nor disasters in the morning." (Psalm 91:5-6) Is that assurance of God's protection? Absolutely! If someone had told me this story, or if I had just read about it, it would not have had the profound impact it did when I actually experienced it myself.

God protected us from the danger on the road. We were not even aware that there was a danger, and isn't that how it usually is? Who plans a disaster or prepares ahead of time for an accident? They come upon us as suddenly and swiftly as those two horses came upon us, but even though we cannot see, God can. Nothing is veiled from Him and He is able to work in our behalf even when our circumstances are totally black.

Psalm 91 became one of my favorite Psalms after this incident. Every verse is filled with the assurance of God's protection. What an answer for the Christian in these troubled and uncertain times when hardly a day passes when a new danger or fear is brought to our attention—horrible, fearful, devastating things—but Praise God!

"We live in the shadow of the Almighty!"

> **"He is close to all who call on Him sincerely.
> He fulfills the desires of those who reverence and trust Him;
> He hears their cries for help and rescues them."
> Psalm 145:18-19**

It was a beautiful sunny day, a perfect day to run errands and keep an appointment that I had in the metro area. It didn't take me long to do everything I had to do, and before long, I was ready for the journey home. Just as I was leaving the establishment I was in, I felt a horrible pain in the small of my back. It hurt so hard I practically saw stars. I'd had back problems in the past, but it had been a long time and I had almost forgotten how awful it could feel. As I tried to take a step, I felt a terrible knifing sensation in my back and my eyes filled with tears. I had no idea how I was I going to drive the 22 miles home.

I began to inch my way to the car. I couldn't stand straight and each step brought incredible pain. The parking lot was in the rear of the building, and I knew that the door I came out of locked behind me. In addition, there was no one around that I could summon for help. No one but the Lord, that is. "Please Lord, help me to get home," were about the only words my pain allowed me to utter.

By the time I got to the car, I was shaking and sweating so hard that my hair was wet and perspiration had started to run down my forehead. The beautiful blue sky and sunshine didn't capture my attention; I hardly noticed it. I only saw the gray cloud that had come over me. It took a lot of doing to ease myself into the driver's seat, and once I got in, I could do nothing but sit there. "Oh, God, please just get me home." Now that I look back, I don't know why I prayed that way. It would have made more sense to ask God to send someone to help me, or to heal me, but all I could think of at the time was the drive ahead and the traffic on the freeway.

I managed to get the key in the ignition and the second I started the car, a voice on the radio blared out, "Christian, why are you sitting there with that backache? Don't you know that Jesus died for that pain and by His stripes you are healed! Lay your hands on your radio and let me pray for you. Claim your healing and your victory!" I did what the voice on the radio said, and in an instant the pain was gone.

When I had gotten out of the car earlier, I had neglected to turn off the radio. I had the volume on very loud so I could hear it over the noise of the freeway traffic. Here, in the quiet parking lot, the sudden blast of a voice at full volume really made an impact—and the Lord's timing was, as usual, perfect! Suddenly, I was aware of the sun again and I felt good all over. I praised the Lord all the way home.

Later, as I thought over everything that had happened, I puzzled over the instant healing. I mentioned that I'd had back problems before, and I have had many back-related issues since, and they have always meant prayer from many people, visits to the chiropractor, physical therapy appointments, medication, and weeks to recover. The Lord definitely blessed me during those times and taught me so much, yet, this time the whole incident took about 20 minutes from the onset of pain to the blast of the radio. "Why, Lord?" I was reminded of a verse in Psalm 91—this was one of the "disasters in the morning" that He took care of. He was my source of strength and He was right there to meet my need. He knew that I needed to be healed instantly.

Sometimes, it only takes an instant to teach me a lesson or Biblical truth because that's what the situation warrants. Many times my prayers had immediate answers. On other occasions, the Lord was doing a different work and needed to keep me down for a while. The Lord uses my "down times" to speak to me—they are the times when He has my full attention.

Wiener Water Soup and Hamburger with Heart

There must be at least 10,000 ways to prepare hamburger, and at one point in my life, I thought I had tried them all. Hamburger was one of the cheapest meats I could buy, and I used it in every fashion I could think of. The one hamburger meal I made most often was just the plain old fashioned "hamburger on a bun."

I had one of those little units that made perfectly round hamburgers every single time. You could cut them out and put them in the round plastic containers, stack them, and pop them into the freezer. One evening, I was in the kitchen preparing my millionth "hamburger on a bun" feast. I had several hamburger patties all thawed and ready for the fry pan. I placed them in the pan—four perfect little circles—and began to cook them.

It was just about that time when the boys came into the kitchen. Tony looked in the pan. "I will not eat another hamburger!" he announced through tears. "Me too," Dave chimed in. I was ready to give my lecture about all the starving of the world who would give anything for a meal like this, but I had a more overpowering feeling to pray instead. "Look, you guys, I know we've been eating a lot of this stuff lately and maybe we're all a little tired of it. Why don't we tell Jesus about it and see if He can help you feel better. " I prayed, asking God to help the kids see that even plain old hamburger could be special when we love Jesus and we are loved by Him. Tony said his prayer, and David added, "Me too."

A few minutes later, Tony came into the kitchen still looking through a few tears. Suddenly he burst out, "Mom! I can't wait to eat tonight! Look at what Jesus made for me!" I turned around and saw Tony pointing at the pan on the stove. I looked and saw that one of the hamburgers was the shape of a perfect heart. Praise the Lord! God can love even through a hamburger.

I had no idea that the day would come when I would be seeing His love through a diet of oatmeal, but a time came when even hamburger was a luxury. The wonderful thing was, we never were hungry and we always had plenty to go around. God always provided and He always blessed us.

One day when we were eating our oatmeal, one of the kids asked how long it would be before we could have a hamburger again. Chet said, "Be thankful for what we have to eat. We could be eating wiener water soup!" "What's that, Dad?" the boys wanted to know. "That's when you have hot dogs one night and you save the water they were cooked in to heat up for supper the next night." "Yuk! And no veggies?" "Nope, guys, no veggies, just the clear soup." Of course he was teasing, but it helped us to see how blessed we were to have the warm oatmeal.

I am thankful for the hamburger and oatmeal days (and the wiener water soup days). They helped us to appreciate the turkey, chops, and steak days when they returned. Once, I put a quart jar of water into the refrigerator with a label on it reading "Wiener Water Soup Stock" as a reminder of how blessed we truly are.

A Work for Me

When we were going through our financial problems, signing up for substitute teaching was one of the ideas we came up with to help us. However, it did not turn out to be the financial boost we were looking for. Every couple of months I made it a point to call the district office to remind them that I was still waiting for a sub position. Each time I called, they assured me that subs were needed and I would be called soon.

I was signed up for an entire year and only received one phone call. I accepted the offer to substitute for three days. The morning I was to go to work I got up early enough to get myself and the boys ready in plenty of time. I had just sent them on their way and was about to leave when the phone rang. It was the principal of the school. She was very sorry, but she would have to cancel the job. She had just learned that I would be subbing in David's classroom and the district policy at that time was that a substitute teacher could not teach in a class where her child was assigned.

At the end of the school year, I called the district office and had my name removed from the sub list. To my surprise, I received a letter from the Superintendent thanking me for being a faithful substitute. He expressed his appreciation for the time I committed to the teachers and students.

The Superintendent's letter was an amusing thing to me at first, but I began to think about all of the people who work in difficult situations day in and day out without getting any recognition, and how often those who do very little, or nothing at all—who know how to manipulate their superiors or leave their work for others to do—are the ones who get the thanks.

We know that the work that we are called to do by our Heavenly Father does not merit an earthly reward, but there will come a day when we will stand before the Lord and be judged for the things we did while we were here. Matthew 25 illustrates this very clearly when Jesus tells the parable of the master and the talents he gave to each of his servants.

Those who were faithful and invested in the master's work were rewarded—"Well done, my good and faithful servant," but the servant who was fearful and did nothing was cast out.

Chet and I talked about my working again and we felt that if subbing wasn't the answer, I should seek employment elsewhere. There was a motel near us and I heard that there were openings for jobs in several different areas. I attended a Bible study with the woman who owned the motel, and I knew I would feel comfortable talking to her. I went to the motel to see her and after we spoke for a while she suggested I fill out an application. I took the paper from her and was about to leave when her husband came into the room. I was totally surprised when he looked at me and said, "You don't want to work here. This is not for you."

Wow! I thought, *he doesn't even know me or know why I am here.* I realized in a moment that the comment had not come from him, but rather was God's way of saying "no" again.

When I came home, I took the phone off the hook and sat down to pray. During my prayer time, I asked the Lord about all that was taking place with the job situation. I had a very strong feeling ever since I came out of the hospital that there was something for me to do. I also had a sense that unless I did it, I would be disobedient to the Lord.

"Lord," I pleaded, "please tell me what it is you want. I won't move from this spot until you tell me what to do."

Finally, He spoke to me. "Mary, I would have you complete the task I assigned to you over a year ago." What task? What in the world was He talking about? Then, a memory flooded into my mind—and it hit me like a ton of bricks—The Book!

A year before, during a time of prayer, the Lord impressed me to write down the things that happened to me since I accepted Jesus as my Lord and Savior. "Begin it as a book." I did write as many things down as I could think of, but slowly, I drifted away from writing until I completely forgot about it. I was stunned that this was what was coming between the Lord and me.

I had not been obedient to what God had told me to do. Words I read in the book *Progress of Another Pilgrim* continued to speak to me on all of this:

> "Let Me teach you how to work in My kingdom. I will fit the task to your capabilities. There is a path of obedience in which you may walk today, a task for which you are prepared, a duty which you may perform for me without fear of failure." [17]

I'm not a writer, and even when I wrote those first experiences down, I looked at it as just a record of what God was doing in my life. Now, I could see that I had taken it lightly. I asked the Lord to give me clear guidance and confirm to me that this was indeed His will. I even went so far as to ask the Lord to let me see or hear the words "the book" and when He showed them to me I asked that they would touch my heart in a way that would erase all doubt. I didn't go searching for the words, I just left it with the Lord and I knew He would answer me.

I didn't have to wait long after my prayer time. I was busy cooking when the phone rang. It was my friend Deb. "What's up with you?" she asked. "Not much. I had quite a time with the Lord today. He is speaking to me about something very specific." Then Deb said, "The book!" I asked her what made her say that and she told me that the words just came into her mind. "Remember, you told me quite a while ago that you were led to keep an account of your walk with Jesus. I think He wants you to write it like a book." I told Deb all that had happened. I had a real case of "spiritual goosebumps" as we talked and after we hung up, I thanked the Lord for answering me in such a way. I shared all of these things with Chet went he came home from work and when I told him that I felt the Lord leading me to start a book, he responded with, "Then, you had better do it!"

Throughout the rest of that evening and into the next day the Lord continued to confirm everything through Scripture and several other sources. The one that impressed me the most was a message from *On the High Road to Surrender*. It read:

> "My words cannot wait; but you have held them up as though you thought the future would wait. Delay no more. Obey me and do so quickly. There is a door open that may soon be shut. There are hearts ready that will be turned in discouragement to error but for your words. Send forth

the message and trust me with its end. I hold all things in my power and I shall direct its going. Hold not back from any seeking soul. Do not analyze the situation, nor seek to protect yourself from misunderstanding nor any words of rejection. Lo, the Spirit accompanies the Word and you may know and be confident that My Spirit anointing the page will bring light and revelation and the confession that God has truly spoken. Yield and Labor. I will add the blessing and the reward. I have called you by name. I have given you My words and I will not have them set aside either by you or by others. Renew your faith. Look directly to Me. I will empower and I will make all things possible as you move in obedience." [18]

I asked the Lord why it had taken so long before He reminded me about writing. He showed me how many lessons I had to learn and how I had to release all to Him and trust Him with everything so I would be free to write. For example, I saw no sense in the subbing experience, but He showed me how that was a life lesson too.

After I had signed up for substitute teaching, I became very disciplined with many of my activities. Things I normally did in the morning (like making the boys' school lunches, picking up toys and newspapers, hanging clothes and doing a general straightening up) I began to do the night before. I would get up the next morning to a practically clean house. I was ready to be called, but I never was, so I went on with the day's activities. The Lord showed me that this is how He wants us to be. We must be prepared for His coming at any time, but we are to carry on with business as usual.

Luke 19:13 instructs the servants to "Occupy until I come".

Mark 13:34: "He laid out their work to do while He was gone and told them to watch for His return."

Mark 13:35-37 tells us to "Keep a sharp lookout! For you do not know when I will come, at evening, at midnight, early dawn or late daybreak. Don't let Me find you sleeping! Watch for My return!"

Luke 12:35-40: "There will be great joy for those who are ready and waiting for His return. The Messiah will come when least expected."

Matthew 24 gives a picture of what it will be like before Jesus comes. In verses 37-39 it explains that "The world will be at ease—banquets, parties and weddings, just as it was in Noah's time before the sudden coming of the flood." People didn't believe what was going to happen until the flood actually arrived and took them away. Verse 42 states, "So be prepared for you don't know what day your Lord is coming."

In Matthew 25 the parable of the ten bridesmaids tells us what will happen to those who are prepared and those who are not prepared when the bridegroom comes. Five were ready and went with him, but the other five were not ready and it was too late for them.

The Lord's task for me was to write down everything He told me to and He would see it through to completion in His time. I needed only to be obedient to Him. In addition, I am to be ready for His coming and if He should tarry, I am to continue to trust and work as He leads.

The Lord did not give me any direction after I had finished writing. That is when I put all of the typed pages into a folder and placed them in a drawer.

Once upon a time, I wrote down all God told me to. I believe in my heart that now is His chosen time to pass it on for others to read.

> "When I think of the wisdom and scope of His plan I fall down on my knees and pray to the Father of all the Family of God, some of them already in Heaven and some down here on earth, that out of His glorious, unlimited resources He will give you the mighty strengthening of His Holy Spirit. And I pray that Christ will be more and more at home in your hearts, living within you as you trust in Him. May your roots go down deep into the soil of God's marvelous love, and may you be able to feel and understand as all God's children should, how long, how wide, how deep and how high His love really is and to experience this love for yourselves, though it is so great that you will never see the end of it or fully know or understand it. And so at last you will be filled up with God Himself.

"Now glory be to God who by His mighty power at work within us is able to do far more than we would ever dare to ask or even dream of—infinitely beyond our highest prayers, desires, thoughts or hopes. May He be given glory forever and ever through endless ages because of His master plan of salvation for the church through Jesus Christ."
Ephesians 3:14-21

It was the middle of July, 2004, when I opened the drawer to discover the things I had written so many years ago. I now felt led to take everything I had recorded on those pages and put it into the stories in this book. When I finished a few weeks later, I asked the Lord for confirmation that it was done as He wanted it to be.

On August 7, 2004, I opened *Grace for the Moment* by Max Lucado and read: "The Master Builder will pull out the original plan and restore it." And, that is exactly what He did!

Amen! Come Lord Jesus!
The grace of the Lord Jesus Christ be with you!
Amen!

Endnotes

1 Roberts, Come Away My Beloved: From Center to Circumference (page 74)

2 Adkins, Thank You for the Dove: What's Wrong With My Children

3 Russell, God Calling by Two Listeners: Deserters (page 172)

4 Rasmussen, The Last Chapter: Removing Spots and Wrinkles (chapter 10)

5 Draper, Living Light

6 Roberts, Come Away My Beloved: The Divine Commission (page 29)

7 Roberts, Come Away My Beloved: Speak the Truth (page 144)

8 Roberts, Come Away My Beloved: Household Salvation (page 58)

9 Roberts, Progress of Another Pilgrim: Recognize My Hand (page 35)

10 Roberts, On the High Road of Surrender: My Spirit Lights the Path (page 69)

11 Roberts, Progress of Another Pilgrim: Be Not Negligent (pages 32-33)

12 Roberts, Come Away My Beloved: A Garden of Fountains (page 63)

13 Roberts, Come Away My Beloved: The Art of Committal (pages 91, 92)

14 Munger, My Heart Christ's Home

15 Wolfe, Whatever It Takes

16 Heil, Lessons from the Furnace

17 Roberts, Progress of Another Pilgrim: Requirements of Discipleship (page 70)

18 Roberts, On the High Road of Surrender: My Words Cannot Wait (page 38)

Works Cited

Adkins, Mike. *Thank You for the Dove.* Mike Adkins Records. Music (Album).

Draper, Edythe (ed.). *Living Light: Messages from the Living Bible.* Illinois: Tyndale House Publishers, 1973. 9th ed.

Heil, Bob. *Lessons from the Furnace.* Harvest Press Incorporated, 1975.

Lucado, Max. *Grace for the Moment.* Tennessee: J. Countryman, a division of Thomas Nelson, Inc., 2000.

Munter, R. B. *My Heart Christ's Home.* Michigan: Meridian, 1989.

Rasmussen, A.W. *The Last Chapter.* Texas: Banner Publishing LLC, 1973.

Roberts, Francis J. *Come Away My Beloved.* California: King's Press, 1964.

Roberts, Francis J. *On the Highroad of Surrender.* California: King's Press, 1973.

Roberts, Francis J. *Progress of Another Pilgrim.* California: King's Press, 1970.

Russell, A.J. (ed.). *God Calling by Two Listeners.* Michigan: Jove Publications, Inc., 2000. 51st ed.

Wolfe, Lanny & Marietta. *Whatever It Takes.* Lanny Wolfe Music, 1975. Song.